Listen In

BOOK
3

Second Edition

David Nunan

HEINLE
CENGAGE Learning

Australia • Brazil • Japan • Korea • Mexico • Singapore • Spain • United Kingdom • United States

HEINLE
CENGAGE Learning™

Listen In 3, Second Edition
David Nunan

Publisher, Global ELT: Christopher Wenger

Editorial Manager: Sean Bermingham

Development Editor: Derek Mackrell

Contributing Editor: Ross Wallace

Production Editor: Tan Jin Hock

ELT Directors: John Lowe (Asia), Jim Goldstone (Latin America-ELT), Francisco Lozano (Latin America-Academic and Training, ELT)

Director of Marketing, EL/ELT: Amy Mabley

Marketing Manager: Ian Martin

Interior/Cover Design: Christopher Hanzie

Illustrations: Raketshop Design Studio, Philippines

Composition: Stella Tan, TYA Inc.

For product information and technology assistance, contact us at
Cengage Learning Customer & Sales Support, 1-800-354-9706

For permission to use material from this text or product,
submit all requests online at **cengage.com/permissions**
Further permissions questions can be emailed to
permissionrequest@cengage.com

ISBN-13: 978-0-8384-0467-6

ISBN-10: 0-8384-0467-7

Heinle
20 Channel Center
Boston, MA 02210
USA

Cengage Learning is a leading provider of customized learning solutions with office locations around the globe, including Singapore, the United Kingdom, Australia, Mexico, Brazil, and Japan. Locate your local office at:
international.cengage.com/region

Cengage Learning products are represented in Canada by Nelson Education, Ltd.

Visit Heinle online at **elt.heinle.com**

Visit our corporate website at **www.cengage.com**

Printed in the United States of America
9 10 11 12 13 14 12 11 10 09

Author's Acknowledgments

First and foremost, I would like to thank Chris Wenger, whose vision for this project matched mine, and who readily understood what I was trying to achieve. Sean Bermingham and Ross Wallace have made a great editorial team, and really took the pain out of the revision process. Heartfelt thanks are also due to the friends, colleagues, and acquaintances who helped in the collection of the authentic data on which the materials are based—you all helped in the creation of a truly special series. Thanks to Dennis Hogan and Tan Tat Chu for their support in paving the way for the second edition, and also to Bob Cullen who astonishes me with his ability to monitor the many projects and initiatives that Thomson Learning has under development.

In addition to the above, I extend my appreciation to the following people, all of whom have helped to make this series a pleasure to work on: Amy Mabley, John Lowe, Ian Martin, Francisco Lozano, Tan Jin Hock, and Derek Mackrell at Thomson Learning; Christopher Hanzie, Stella Tan, and the staff at T.Y.A.; Leo Cultura and the staff at Raketshop Design Studio.

I am also very grateful to the following professionals who provided invaluable comments and suggestions during the development of this series:

Brett Bowie — Konkuk University, Korea
Marlene Brenes — Benemerita University, Mexico
Grace Chang — Tak Ming College, Taiwan
Grace Chao — Soochow University, Taiwan
Jim Chou — National Chengchi University, Taiwan
Susana Christie — San Diego State University, USA
Karen Cisney — Soochow University, Taiwan
Carla Diez — ITESM, Mexico
Michael Fox — Seoul National University of Education, Korea
Chiu-hua Fu — Van Nung Institute of Technology, Taiwan
Pierre Gauvin — Sung Dong ECC, Korea
Frank Graziani — Tokai University, Japan
Ann-Marie Hadzima — National Taiwan University, Taiwan
Patti Hedden — Yonsei University, Korea
Angela Hou — Fu-Jen Catholic University, Taiwan
Yu-chen Hso — Soochow University, Taiwan
Ju-ying Vinia Huang — Tamkang University, Taiwan
Yuko Iwata — Tokai University, Japan
Inga Jelescheff — Saguragaoka High School, Japan
Monica Kamio — AEON Amity, Japan
Alexis Kim — English City Institute, Korea
Mia Kim — Kyunghee University, Korea
Jane King — Soochow University, Taiwan
Mary Ying-hsiu Ku — Taipei Municipal First Girl's High School, Taiwan
Balk-eum Lee — Aju University Education Center, Korea
Cheri Lee — One World Language Institute, Korea
Jenny Lee — Seoul National University of Education, Korea
Li-te Li — Tung Fang B & E Vocational High School, Taiwan

Jui-hsiang Lu — Van Nung Institute of Technology, Taiwan
Shiona MacKenzie — Gakashuin Boys' Senior High School, Japan
Rhona McCrae — Freelance English Instructor, Japan
Michael Noonan — Kookmin University, Korea
Maria Ordoñez — Universidad de Celaya, Mexico
Daisy Pan — Van Nung Institute of Technology, Taiwan
Jason Park — Korea University of Foreign Studies, Korea
Young Park — Dankook University, Korea
Kerry Read — Blossom English Center, Japan
Lesley Riley — Kanazawa Institute of Technology, Japan
Cathy Rudnick — Hanyang University, Korea
Kathy Sherak — San Francisco State University, USA
Yoshiko Shimizu — Osaka College of Foreign Languages, Japan
John Smith — International Osaka Owada Koko, Japan
Sue Sohn — Sung Dong ECC, Korea
May Tang — National Taiwan University, Taiwan
Yu-hsin Tsai — Chinese Culture University, Taiwan
Melanie Vandenhoeven — Sungshin University, Korea
Holly Winber — Senzoku Gakuen Fuzoku Koko, Japan
Jane Wu — Fu-Jen Catholic University, Taiwan
Hsiao-tsui Yang — Shih Chien University, Taiwan
Hai-young Yun — Korea Development Institute, Korea

Scope and Sequence

Unit	Title/Topic	Goals	Sources	Pronunciation
Starter *Page 8*	*Using listening strategies.* **Listening skills**	Identifying listening strategies	Casual conversations Sales presentation Lecture	Identifying words in rapid speech
1 *Page 12*	*He's the generous type.* **Personal qualities**	Understanding personal qualities	Casual conversations Monologs Questionnaire survey	Identifying word stress in sentences
2 *Page 16*	*We could get him a tie.* **Gift-giving**	Understanding reasons Evaluating information	Monologs Casual conversations	Identifying contractions of *'d* and *'ll*
3 *Page 20*	*What exactly do you do?* **Job responsibilities**	Understanding job descriptions Identifying job responsibilities	Job descriptions Interviews Monolog	Assimilation: *would you, meet you*
4 *Page 24*	*It doesn't fit.* **Clothes and fashion**	Understanding complaints Distinguishing between fact and opinion	Monologs Casual conversation Store conversation	Linking: consonant-consonant
5 *Page 28*	*I'm not sure what it's called.* **Household items**	Understanding descriptions of everyday objects Understanding vague descriptions	Household conversations	Stress for asking for repetition
1–5 *Page 32*	**Review**		Job descriptions Store conversation Casual conversations	
6 *Page 34*	*I thought you spoke English!* **Types of English**	Distinguishing between varieties of English Following an academic lecture	Lecture Hotel conversation Tour guide talk	Identifying different accents
7 *Page 38*	*You'll buy anything.* **Advertisements**	Understanding ad messages Recognizing approval and disapproval	Advertisements Casual conversation Lecture	Elision: *don't need*
8 *Page 42*	*Our sales target is $1.1 million.* **Business**	Identifying large numbers Understanding business data	News reports Sales presentations Office conversation	Intrusion: *be able*
9 *Page 46*	*I have a driving lesson tonight.* **Driving**	Understanding sequence of events Identifying information on the telephone	Telephone conversations Voice messages Casual conversations Instructional talk	Identifying and understanding fillers
10 *Page 50*	*She wants a seat to Miami.* **Travel**	Understanding travel plans Identifying schedule information	Telephone conversations Automated phone system	Weak forms: overview
6–10 *Page 54*	**Review**		Sales presentations Casual conversations Car advertisements	

Unit	Title/Topic	Goals	Sources	Pronunciation
11 *Page 56*	*How do I get downtown?* **Directions**	Understanding directions Understanding telephone conversations	Telephone conversations Street conversations Hotel conversation	Linking: final consonant-initial vowel
12 *Page 60*	*Is this where I get my student ID?* **On campus**	Identifying purpose Following a sequence of events	Conversation on campus Bureaucratic conversations Telephone conversation	Assimilation: *have to, has to, used to*
13 *Page 64*	*It's a really cool site.* **The Internet**	Understanding opinions Identifying frequency	Casual conversations Lecture	Intrusion: *go_won*
14 *Page 68*	*That's a good question.* **Talk shows**	Understanding interviews and talk shows Identifying advantages and disadvantages	TV broadcasts Talk show Interviews at a studio	Strong and weak forms of *that*
15 *Page 72*	*Do you have a pet peeve?* **Peeves and phobias**	Understanding interviews Identifying solutions	TV interview Casual conversations	Intrusion: the *idea₁is*
11–15 *Page 76*	**Review**		Monologs TV talk show Interview	
16 *Page 78*	*That sounds dangerous!* **Adventure**	Identifying attitude Following instructions	Casual conversations Instructional talk	Intonation for sarcasm
17 *Page 82*	*It has good points and bad points.* **Conservation**	Identifying arguments for and against an issue Listening critically to alternative viewpoints	Casual conversations Radio talk show	Assimilation: *whacha think?*
18 *Page 86*	*I was so embarrassed.* **Feelings**	Following a narrative Identifying feelings and emotions	Monologs	Weak forms: pronouns
19 *Page 90*	*What's on TV tonight?* **Television**	Identifying the topic of a monolog Following instructions	TV broadcasts Instructional talk Casual conversation	Intonation to show enthusiasm
20 *Page 94*	*I hear what you're saying.* **The senses**	Understanding a scientific explanation Following an academic lecture	Academic lectures	Elision: *cup of tea*
16–20 *Page 98*	**Review**		Monologs Casual conversations TV show previews	

To the Student

Dear Student,

Welcome to *Listen In*. This three-level series will give you many opportunities to develop your listening skills. It will also help you improve your speaking skills. There are several important features of the series that may be unfamiliar to you. They include real-life tasks, real-life language, and learning strategies.

Real-life tasks
The tasks you do in *Listen In* are all based on the kinds of listening that you do in real life, such as following directions, listening to telephone messages, and understanding the news and weather.

Real-life language
The listening materials are also taken from real life. You will hear many different kinds of recorded language, including conversations, telephone messages, store announcements, news and weather broadcasts, and public announcements.

Learning strategies
In addition to teaching you language, *Listen In* also focuses on learning strategies. In completing the tasks, you will use strategies that will improve your listening inside and outside the classroom.

Each level of *Listen In* consists of a Starter Unit to get you thinking about the listening strategies in the book, as well as giving you some practice using those strategies. There are 20 main units and four Review units. Linked to each of the main units is a page of Self-Study Practice at the back of the book. Here is what each unit contains:

Warm-up Task

This section is designed to introduce you to the topic for the unit and present some of the important vocabulary and expressions that you will hear and eventually use in the unit.

Listening Tasks

You will then hear a number of different listening passages, all of which relate to the target language of that unit. One of the listening tasks in each unit focuses on pronunciation; another type of task allows you to decide on your own response. The *Listen for it* boxes highlight useful words and expressions commonly used in everyday speech. The teacher will ask you to listen to most passages more than once. This will give you the chance to understand more of what you hear, use a variety of listening strategies, and check your answers to the listening tasks.

Your Turn!

The last page gives you the opportunity to practice the target language you have been listening to. *Try this . . .* is a communicative task that you complete in pairs or in groups. The sample language in the box will help you to complete this task. *In Focus* gives you cultural information that you can discuss as a class.

Self-Study Practice

After class, you can get extra listening practice by turning to the back of the book (pages 107–127) and completing the Self-Study Practice Units.

The main thing to remember when you are using these materials is to relax and enjoy yourself as you learn. In some units, you will hear conversations in which you will not understand every word. This does not matter. Not even native English speakers understand or listen for every single word. This series will help you develop strategies for understanding the most important information.

I had a great time creating *Listen In*. I hope that you enjoy using these materials as much as I enjoyed writing them.

Good luck!

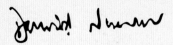

Classroom Language

Could you repeat that, please?

Could you play it again, please?

Could you turn up the volume, please?

How do you say . . . in English?

What does . . . mean?

How do you spell . . . ?

I'm not sure.

Sorry, I don't understand.

What did you get for question number one?

What's your answer for number two?

Using listening strategies.

Goals
• Identifying listening strategies

Different kinds of listening tasks involve different kinds of listening strategies. Sometimes we need to listen for gist, or for the main idea. In some cases we need to infer information that is not said directly.

A Listen and number the situations (1–8) in the order you hear them.

Has Brad done this procedure before?

a. Yes. **b.** No.

The woman is being given directions to . . .

a. someone's office. **b.** someone's house.

The two speakers . . .

a. are friends. **b.** have just met.

Does the man like classical music?

a. Yes. **b.** No.

The speakers are talking about . . .
a. someone they know well.
b. someone they don't know well.

How does the speaker feel about the company's performance?
a. He's happy. b. He's unhappy.

The woman is applying for a position as . . .
a. designer. b. finance officer.

What subject is this class?
a. Mathematics. b. History.

B **Listen again. Circle the correct answer under each photo.**

Another strategy is listening for purpose, i.e., trying to understand the speaker's intention. When we listen, we may not hear or understand every word, so guessing and predicting are also useful strategies to use.

 A **Listen. What is the speaker doing? Circle the purpose of each statement.**

Purpose	Your response
1. apologizing / introducing	_____
2. offering / requesting	_____
3. inviting / giving directions	_____
4. complimenting / criticizing	_____
5. introducing / accepting	_____
6. suggesting / inviting	_____

B **Listen again. Predict what the next speaker will say. Write your response. Then listen to hear how the other person responded.**

Using listening strategies.

3 *When people speak quickly, the pronunciation of individual words, and groups of words, can change from their pronunciation in slower speech. Being able to recognize what is being said in fast speech is an important skill.*

A Listen. Write the sentences you hear.

1. _____
2. _____
3. _____
4. _____
5. _____
6. _____

B Listen again and check your answers.

4 *Sometimes we need to listen for the most important pieces of information. The next two tasks involve listening for key details, first in a lecture, and then in a conversation.*

A Listen to the lecture. Number the listening strategies in the order the lecturer mentions them.

Strategies	Examples
_____ asking for repetition	_____
_____ asking for clarification	_____
_____ listening for key words	_____

B Listen again. Give examples of each strategy.

5

A Listen to Kim and Tina talking about their listening class. What problems does Tina have?

Problem	Suggested strategy
_____	_____
_____	_____
_____	_____

B Listen again. What strategy does Kim suggest for each problem? Write the number from Task 4.

Your Turn!

Talking about types of listening

- As soon as I woke up I **turned on the radio and listened to the news.**
- Then I was **listening for key details**—I wanted to find out the sports results.
- Later on, **my brother was telling me a long story,** and I was **trying to understand the sequence of events.**
- Later in the day, I was **chatting with friends. It was pretty noisy,** so I had to **keep asking them to repeat what they were saying.**
- This morning I was just **listening for the general ideas of a lecture,** I wasn't really **listening for details.**

Listening in my language

_____
_____
_____
_____
_____
_____

Listening in English

_____
_____
_____
_____
_____
_____
_____
_____

Try this . . .

Work with a partner. How many types of listening (in your first language) have you listened to since you woke up this morning? Make a list. What skills or strategies did you use for each one? Make a similar list for English. Discuss with your partner.

In Focus: _Why is listening so difficult?_

Most learners would agree that listening in English can be difficult at times. What is it that makes some listening tasks more difficult than others? Research has shown that there are four factors that contribute to the difficulty of a listening task: **speaker** factors—including the number of speakers, how quickly they speak, and their type of accent; **listener** factors—whether the listener is simply overhearing another conversation or is able to join in, and how much the learner knows about the topic and how interested they are in it; **support**—for example, are there diagrams, pictures, or other visual clues to help; and the **content** of the listening—how difficult is the grammar and vocabulary, and what background knowledge of the topic does the learner need. Also, listening is easier when information is presented in the same order as it occurred in real life. _Is listening in English difficult for you? What factors do you think can make listening difficult?_

I really find listening to technical language difficult. There are too many words I don't know.

Listening to English would be a lot easier if everyone spoke a bit more slowly.

I'm OK when it's just one person, but listening to a group is tough for me.

Using listening strategies.

11

He's the generous type.

Goals • Understanding personal qualities

①

A How would you describe the people below? Write a word to complete each sentence.

| aggressive | selfish | kind | impatient | jealous | generous |

Hilary is _I_____

Ron is _G_____

Jim is _A_____

Lucy is _K_____

Pat is _J_____

Kyle is _S_____

B Who do you think is saying each of these things? Write the name of the person next to each quote.

Quote	Speaker
"When he wants something, he really goes out and gets it!"	_____
"I don't want to share! It's mine!"	_____
"Excuse me, ma'am. Why don't you sit down here?"	_____
"He's having lunch with Jennifer. Again!"	_____
"Can't we go any faster?"	_____
"Mark couldn't use his, so he gave them to me."	_____

C **Brainstorm!** Work with a partner. What are some other words that can be used to describe personality? Make a list.

2

A Listen and number the pictures (1–6) in Task 1 in the order you hear them.

B Listen again and read the statements. Circle *T* for *True*, *F* for *False,* or *U* for *Unknown*.

1. Jim Stockdale is a successful businessman.   T   F   U
2. Kyle's sister always shares her candy with him.   T   F   U
3. The young woman is getting off the bus at the next stop.   T   F   U
4. Pat's friend doesn't believe that Scott and Jennifer are having lunch together.   T   F   U
5. The woman in the car is going to a meeting that starts in 20 minutes.   T   F   U
6. Mark is taking a friend to the basketball game.   T   F   U

3

A What qualities do the speakers like and dislike?
Listen and fill in the chart.

> **Listen for it**
>
> A *quirk* is an odd or unusual habit or personality characteristic.

Speaker	Likes people who are . . .	Dislikes people who are . . .
Dora		
Keith		
Michelle		

B Listen again and check your answers.

He's the generous type. **13**

4

A Cindy is answering a magazine survey with her boyfriend. Listen and check (✔) the correct column.

Hit the roof is an idiom meaning to become very angry.

	Extremely	Very	Sort of	Not very	Not at all
Aggressive		✔			
Selfish				✔	
Kind					
Patient			✔		
Jealous		✔			

B Listen again. In what situations has Cindy been . . . ?

aggressive *when she drives*   kind _____   jealous _____

selfish _____   impatient _____

5

A Listen. Which word is stressed? Check (✔) the sentence you hear.

1. Why can't you be a little more patient with **me**? ☐
   Why can't **you** be a little more patient with me? ☐
   Why can't you be a little more **patient** with me? ☑

2. **I** said Cheryl is not the aggressive type. ☐
   I said Cheryl is not the **aggressive** type. ☐
   I said **Cheryl** is not the aggressive type. ☑

3. You don't think I was being **selfish**, do you? ☑
   You don't think I was being selfish, do you? ☐
   You don't think **I** was being selfish, do you? ☐

4. I am **not** jealous of her. ☑
   I am not jealous of **her**. ☐
   I am not jealous of her. ☐

5. You're being a bit **too** kind. ☐
   You're being **a bit** too kind. ☐
   You're being a bit too kind. ☐

6. Try to be **more** generous to him. ☐
   Try to be more generous to him. ☑
   Try to be more generous to **him**. ☐

B Listen again and practice.

6

Listen and circle the answers that are right for you.

1. Yes, I am.   Oh, sort of, I guess.   No, I'm not.
2. No, I wouldn't.   Not really.   Yes, I would.
3. Oh, extremely.   Yes, I am.   No, not very.
4. Yes, very!   No, not very.   No, not at all.
5. Yes, extremely.   Sort of, I guess.   No, not very.
6. No, I hate it.   I don't really mind.   Actually, I do.

Your Turn! 🔊

Asking and answering questions about personality traits

- What kinds of people do you like most?
  I really like people who are **adventurous** and **outgoing**.
  I prefer people who are **thoughtful** and **caring**.
- What qualities don't you like in a person?
  I can't stand people who **don't listen**.
  It drives me crazy when people **get impatient**.
- What's your best friend like?
  He's a really **generous** guy. I once **saw him give $20 to a homeless person on the street**.
- How do you feel about **aggressive** people?
  I really **hate** people who **can't control their temper**.

Personal Qualities

➕ _____
_____
_____
_____
_____

➖ _____
_____
_____
_____
_____
_____

Try this . . .

What qualities do you like most in a person? What qualities do you dislike? Make a list of at least three for each and share them with a partner. Explain why you like or dislike each quality. Answer your partner's questions.

In Focus: *She's not my type*

For centuries, attempts have been made to assign people to simple, easy-to-define categories. The most common of these are the signs of the zodiac, both Western and Asian, but another common one is blood types. According to this theory each of the four blood types has its own personality characteristics. Type A people are calm, polite, shy, and sensitive. Type B are practical, serious, and individualistic. Type AB are unique, trustworthy, and responsible, while Type O people are outgoing, energetic, and social. Renowned psychologist Carl Jung also classified people into one of four categories: "Rationals" such as Albert Einstein, "Idealists" such as Mahatma Gandhi, "Artisans" such as Leonardo da Vinci, and "Guardians" such as England's Queen Elizabeth I. *What's your opinion of theories that seek to classify people into a limited number of "types"? If you had to choose a category for yourself based on Jung's categories, which would it be? Why?*

He's the generous type.

UNIT 2

We could get him a tie.

Goals • Understanding reasons
• Evaluating information

1

A Read the list of occasions on which people typically give gifts. Add at least four more occasions to the list.

birthday	housewarming	_____
wedding	graduation	_____
anniversary	_____	_____

B Look at the photos. Who would you give these gifts to, and for what occasion? Discuss with a partner.

C **Brainstorm!** Work with a partner. Make lists of brand names, models, and descriptions (where appropriate) for at least three of the gifts above.

A Listen. Which of the gifts in Task 1 are the people talking about? Write the gift for each.

Gift	Key words
1.	
2.	
3.	
4.	
5.	

B Listen again and write the key words that helped you decide.

3

A What are the people planning? Listen and check (✔) the correct column.

Listen for it

Lost touch is an informal way of saying you haven't spoken to a relative or friend for a long time.

	Possibly	Probably not
A wedding anniversary party		
A graduation party		
An engagement party		
A birthday party		

B Listen again. Are these people invited or not? Circle the correct answer and write the reason.

Guest	Invited?	Reason
Uncle Ferdie	Yes Not sure No	
The Homans	Yes Not sure No	
Cousin Henry	Yes Not sure No	

We could get him a tie. **17**

4

A
Look at the example sentences and listen. What is *'ll* short for? What is *'d* short for?

> **Example:** Look at this. John'd love it.   *Look at this. John'll love it.*

B
Listen and check (✔) the sentence you hear.

1. Oh, I think I'd buy him a tie. ☑
  Oh, I think I'll buy him a tie. ☐

2. Those colors'd suit you better. ☐
  Those colors'll suit you better. ☐

3. I'd need to get him a present. ☐
  I'll need to get him a present. ☐

4. Do you think he'll like it? ☐
  Do you think he'd like it? ☐

5. Yes, those ties'd really suit him. ☐
  Yes, those ties'll really suit him. ☐

6. Do you think it'll fit Paula? ☐
  Do you think it'd fit Paula? ☐

C
Listen again and practice. When does the speaker use *'ll*, and when does the speaker use *'d*?

5

A
Some family members are discussing which gift to buy for their father. Listen and write the gifts that they reject.

Listen for it
If something is *out of your league* it's too expensive or too difficult for you.

Rejected gift	Why was it rejected?
1.	
2.	
3.	
4.	
5.	

B
Why do they reject the gifts? Listen again and write the reason.
What do they finally decide to buy? _____

6

Listen and circle the answers that are right for you.

1. Sure, why not?	It depends who it was for.	No way.
2. I think it is.	Some people might think so.	No, I don't think so.
3. Sounds good to me.	I suppose it's OK.	It's not really appropriate.
4. Very important.	Kind of important.	Not very important.
5. I'm all for it.	I might do it.	I don't like the idea.
6. Yes, I would.	It's possible.	No, I wouldn't.

Your Turn! 🔊

Making choices and giving reasons

- So, what should we get for **Julia**?
  I think we should buy her a **DVD**. I've heard **she collects them**.
- **Evelyn** is always **complaining that she's cold**. We could get her a **cardigan**.
  That's a good idea. She'd like that.
  I don't know about that. She's pretty **choosy about her clothes**.
- What do you think about **sunglasses** for **Ray**?
  Yeah, he'd look **really cool in them**.
  No, **I doubt he'd ever wear them**.
- Which do you think she'd like better—a **handbag** or **a pair of shoes**?
  Let's go with the **handbag**. She's already got **a lot of shoes**.

Try this . . .

Work with a partner. Choose two classmates and make separate lists of birthday gifts that would be suitable for each. Give reasons for your gift choices and decide together which one would be most appropriate for each person.

Name: _____

Gift ideas: _____

_____

_____

Name: _____

Gift ideas: _____

_____

_____

In Focus: *Getting more than you give*

Once a symbol of success, the crooked "E" logo of the Enron Corporation took on a new meaning in the aftermath of the U.S. energy giant's collapse in 2001. In what was at the time the biggest bankruptcy in American history, Enron toppled under the weight of $3 billion in debt resulting from corrupt accounting practices and simple greed. Besides causing untold millions of dollars in losses to employees and investors, the Enron scandal left many colleges, museums, politicians, and charities on the company's donation list wondering whether they were the beneficiaries of ill-gotten money. Many recipients of donations decided to keep the cash, while others returned it—in some cases out of a sense of duty and in others due to public pressure. *What would you do if you learned a gift you had received was stolen? Would you do the same thing if no one else knew it was stolen? In which situations would you consider it wrong to accept a gift?*

I don't see anything wrong with keeping a stolen gift. It's not like I stole it.

I'd be ashamed to keep a stolen gift. I'd try to return it to its rightful owner.

As a journalist, I'm not supposed to accept gifts of any kind. It's unethical.

We could get him a tie.

 19

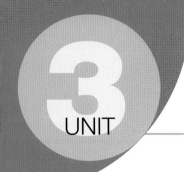

What exactly do you do?

Goals
- Understanding job descriptions
- Identifying job responsibilities

1

A Look at the jobs in the box and match them to the correct person in the TV studio. One job is extra.

camera operator   sound engineer   director   newscaster

makeup artist   producer   lighting technician

B What do the people in the picture do? Combine items from the boxes below to describe their job responsibilities.

do   make   check   operate   supervise   control   read   write   manage

research	the lights	employees	decisions
the camera	scripts	the studio	planning

C **Brainstorm!** Work with a partner. Make a list of other jobs. What are the job responsibilities for each of these jobs? Use the words above, or other words.

editor—do research, . . .

A **Listen to six people from the TV studio talking about their jobs. What is each person's job?**

Listen for it

Make sure (that) is commonly used to mean check or ensure.

Job	Key words
1.	
2.	
3.	
4.	
5.	
6.	

B **Listen again. What keywords helped you decide?**

3

A **Listen to an interview with three people. What are Henry, Janelle, and Rob's jobs?**

Name	Job	Responsibilities
Henry Long		
Janelle Lee		
Rob Martello		

B **Listen again. What are each person's job responsibilities?**

4

A **Listen to six statements and questions. For each one, circle the correct function.**

1. offer	request	**4.** suggest	offer
2. introduce	compliment	**5.** question	introduce
3. inform	introduce	**6.** suggest	invite

5

A Look at the example sentence, and listen to the way the /t/ and /y/ sounds combine to make a /ch/ sound.

> **Example:** It's great to meet you.

B Look at the following sentences and circle where you think the sounds will change. Listen and check your answers.

1. Why don't you tell him what you do?
2. Where did you go on the weekend?
3. Is that the dog that bit you?
4. What would you like to know?
5. Why didn't you give me a call?
6. Had you ever been there before?

C Listen again. Now, practice saying the sentences with a partner.

6

A Donna is head of recruitment at a TV studio. Listen to her give advice to applicants, and check (✔) the things she talks about.

☐ preparation	☐ clothing	☐ experience	☐ attitude
☐ punctuality	☐ body language	☐ résumé	☐ strengths and weaknesses

B Listen again and note her five pieces of advice.

1. _____
2. _____
3. _____
4. _____
5. _____

7

Listen and circle the answers that are right for you.

1. Yeah, I'd love to!   It would be OK.   No, not at all.
2. They sure do.   A little, I guess.   I don't mind them.
3. Salary.   Interest.   They're both important.
4. Work for myself.   A company.   I don't mind either way.
5. No way!   No, but I'd buy a company.   Of course!

Your Turn! 🔊

Talking about job responsibilities

- What do you do?
- What do you do for a living?
  I'm **an accountant**.
  I **drive a truck**.
  I **work for a TV studio**.
- What do you do at work?
- What does your job involve?
- What are your job responsibilities?
  I **do research** and **help write scripts**.
  I **manage the lights and sound**.
  I **check the sound levels** and **make sure the lights are OK**.

Job: _____
Responsibilities: _____
_____
_____
_____
_____
_____
_____
_____

Try this . . .

Think of a job and the responsibilities for that job, and write them in the chart. Find other students and ask them about their jobs and job responsibilities. Answer their questions. Who has the most interesting job?

In Focus: *All work and no play*

Do you think that workers in your country work long hours? A recent study found workers in the United States worked more hours per week than almost anyone else in the industrialized world. The study by the United Nations' International Labor Organization found that the average American worked 1,978 hours a year. That's about 100 hours a year more than the average Australian, Canadian, Japanese, or Mexican worker, 250 hours a year more than Brazilian and British workers, and almost 500 hours a year more than German workers. According to the study, the hardest-working employees in the world are the South Koreans, who worked an average of 500 hours a year more than the Americans. This increase in working hours by Americans (up 2 percent in the last decade) has led to criticism that personal time is being overtaken by work. *Do people work hard in your country? Is working hard a good thing? What (if anything) would you do to change the number of hours people work?*

I think people in my country do a lot of overtime, but they're not really working.

People used to work a lot harder in the past than they do now.

I'd like to see twice as many public holidays every year.

What exactly do you do?

It doesn't fit.

Goals
• Understanding complaints
• Distinguishing between fact and opinion

1

A **Label the pictures, using the words in the box.**

| hem | collar | buttons | stitching | sleeve | waist | zipper |

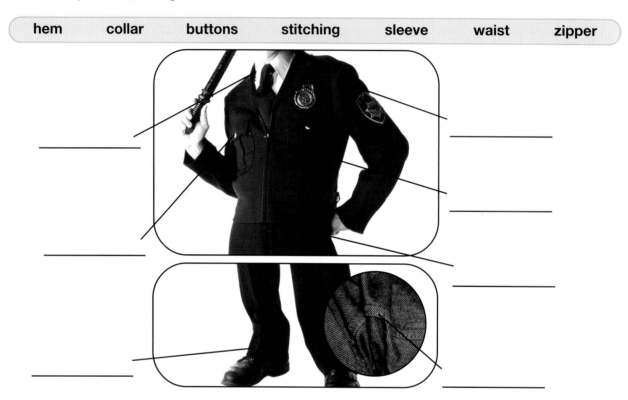

B **What's wrong in each picture below? Use one word or expression from each box to complete the sentences.**

| hem | stitching | button | zipper | | come off | come down | come undone | broken |

The _____ is
_____.

The _____
has _____.

The _____ is
about to _____.

The _____
has _____.

C **Brainstorm! What would you wear on each of these occasions: Your graduation ceremony? Your grandparents' wedding anniversary? Going to the movies? A job interview? A picnic? Discuss with a partner.**

2

A Listen. What are the people complaining about? Number the items 1–4.

 ○ 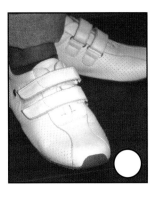 ○  ○  ○

B Listen again. What's wrong with each item? Write the complaint.

Complaint
1.
2.
3.
4.

3

A Vanessa and Kathy are shopping. Listen to their conversation and fill in the missing words. Is each statement a fact or an opinion? Check (✔) the correct column.

	Fact	Opinion
1. The _____ looks great on Vanessa.		
2. _____ don't look right on Vanessa.		
3. Vanessa couldn't wear _____ to her brother's wedding.		
4. Vanessa would be happy in _____ and a _____.		

B Listen again and check your answers.
What are Vanessa and Kathy going to do now? _____

4

A Listen to the rest of Vanessa and Kathy's conversation and answer the questions.

1. What is Vanessa trying to do? _____

2. What's wrong with the dress? _____

3. What's the salesperson going to do? _____

B Listen again and check your answers. Discuss with a partner: What do you think the manager will say?

It doesn't fit.   **25**

5

A Look at the example sentence, and listen to the way the two /t/ sounds merge to make one slightly longer sound.

> **Example.** Why do you want to return it?

B Look at the following sentences, and circle where you predict that two consonant sounds will merge. Listen and check your answers.

1. I never really liked disco.
2. I bought two ties last Tuesday.
3. Did you buy a new watch?

4. That's Steve over there. Next to his sister.
5. I need Don to give me some money.
6. Have you seen Neil's new black cap?

C Listen again. Now, practice saying the sentences with a partner.

6

A Listen to the statements. Is each statement a compliment or a criticism? Check (✔) the correct column.

	Compliment	Criticism	Responses	
1.			Thanks, it's new.	Oh no, it's ugly.
2.			Thanks a lot.	You don't like it?
3.			Be quiet.	You're right, I'll change them.
4.			Oh, I'll get another one.	Yeah, I think so too.
5.			You don't like it?	It's beautiful, isn't it?
6.			Yeah, I got them yesterday.	Thanks, very much.

B Listen again and circle the best response.

7

Listen and circle the answers that are right for you.

1. Yes, definitely.   I guess so.   No, it's not important to me.
2. I sure am.   I'm not bad.   No, I'm kind of scruffy.
3. I love it.   Sometimes.   No, not at all.
4. Yeah, too much.   A fair amount.   No, hardly anything.
5. I only buy brand names. It depends on the item. No, they don't mean anything.

Your Turn! 🔊

Talking about clothes and fashion

- What do you think?
  It **looks great!**
  It **fits perfectly!**
  It **doesn't look right on you.**
  It **doesn't really suit you.**
- That **dress** looks great on you.
  Thanks.
- Can I help you, sir?
  Yeah, I wonder if I could exchange these, please?
- Sure, what's the problem?
  They're **too tight.**
  The **hem's come down.**
  A **button's come off.**
  The **stitching is coming undone.**
  They're **the wrong size.**

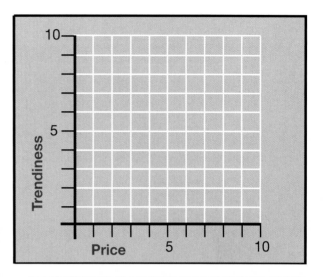

Try this . . .

With a partner, make a list of six brand names you know. Write the names on the graph, according to how expensive and trendy they are. Show your graph to another pair and discuss your choices.

In Focus: *What's in a name?*

When Louis Vuitton, the luxury handbag maker, opened a new store in Tokyo in 2002, people queued for hours to get in, and the store sold $1 million worth of handbags on the first day. Why is this brand so successful? The success of Louis Vuitton depends on a number of factors. The company uses a luxury pricing strategy, using high markups, limited availability, and few markdowns to keep the image exclusive. The company president says "no" to after-Christmas sales: "They would devalue the brand." Also Louis Vuitton only sells its products through its own stores (284 worldwide in 2002), enabling the company to keep control of image and quality at every stage. The company's strategy is a successful one—in the 150 years since the Louis Vuitton company started as a leather goods manufacturer in Paris, it has grown to be the largest worldwide seller of fashion and leather goods. *Do you own any brand name products? Why do you think certain brand names are so successful?*

I like brand name products because they're good quality, not just because they're fashionable.

People buy brand name items because they want to follow the crowd.

People today are so worried about image. That's why brand names are so popular.

It doesn't fit. **27**

I'm not sure what it's called.

Goals • Understanding descriptions of everyday objects
• Understanding vague descriptions

1

A Label the pictures with the items below, then write a word to complete each definition.

_____ _____ _____ _____

_____ _____ _____ _____

Item	It's used for . . .
frying pan	making _____
corkscrew	opening _____
chopsticks	picking up _____
kettle	boiling _____

Item	It's used for . . .
can opener	opening cans of _____
potholder	holding hot _____
spatula	flipping _____ in a pan.
cutting board	cutting _____

B Choose an item from the list and describe it to your partner, without saying what it is. Your partner will guess. Think of other items and ask your partner to guess.

C **Brainstorm!** Work with a partner. What other items can you find in a kitchen? Make a list. Plan your dream kitchen. What items would you like to have in it?

2

A Listen to five conversations. What objects are they talking about?

Item	Key words
1.	
2.	
3.	
4.	
5.	

B Listen again and write the keywords that helped you decide.

3

A Two students are sharing an apartment. What are they buying for their kitchen? Listen and check (✔) the correct list.

Shopping List:
frying pan
chopsticks
corkscrew
potholder
cutting board

Shopping List:
frying pan
spatula
kettle
can opener
corkscrew

Shopping List:
potholder
can opener
spatula
frying pan
chopsticks

B Listen again and check your answers.

4

A Listen and circle the best response.

1. It's called a spatula.   It's for flipping eggs and stuff.

2. Chopsticks? They're easy to use.   I use chopsticks.

3. Yes, I have a corkscrew.   It's called a corkscrew.

4. The kettle's on the stove.   Oh, you mean a kettle.

5. A cutting board? OK, fine.   I forget what it's called.

B Listen again and check your answers.

I'm not sure what it's called.

5

A Read the statements 1–4. Listen to the conversation between Michelle and Anne and circle *T* for *True*, *F* for *False*, or *U* for *Unknown*.

1. Michelle is going to university.	T	F	U
2. Michelle and Anne lived together.	T	F	U
3. Anne is going to France too.	T	F	U
4. Michelle is from France.	T	F	U

B Listen again and note who gets each item. On the list, write A for the items Anne gets, and M for the ones Michelle gets.

kettle
can opener
frying pan
cutting board
spatula
corkscrew
pot holder
chopsticks

6

A Listen to the example exchange and note how the speaker uses stress on the *Wh-* word (*What*) to ask the other person to repeat information.

> **Example:**
> **A:** What is this called?
> **B:** It's called a cutting board.
>
> **A:** **What** is it called?
> **B:** A cutting board.

B Listen and check (✔) the questions that are asking someone to repeat information.

1. What are they called? ☐

2. What are these things called? ☐

3. What's that on the table? ☐

4. What is it used for? ☐

5. Who bought that for you? ☐

6. When did you get it? ☐

C Work with a partner. Practice these sentences following the example.

7

Listen and circle the answers that are right for you

1. Of course, I use them every day.	Yeah, I'm not bad.	No, not really.
2. Yeah, I'm pretty good.	I'm OK.	No, I'm terrible.
3. Men.	Women.	There's no difference.
4. I agree.	Maybe, but not in my house.	No way!

Your Turn! 🔊

Describing everyday objects

- What's that thing over there called?
  Hmm. I'm not sure.
- What's this thing used for?
  It's used for **cutting food**.
- Do you know what it's called?
  It's called **a cutting board**.
- Do you know how to use these things?
  Chopsticks? Sure, I'll show you.
- I want to buy one of those things for **boiling water**.
  Oh, you mean **a kettle**?

Try this . . .

Work with a partner. You and your partner are going to be sharing a semi-furnished apartment. It has beds, a fridge, and a washing machine, but nothing else. You have $2,000 to spend between you. Look at the list of items and prices, and decide with your partner what you are going to buy. Compare with another pair.

Television $300
Stereo $250
Computer $900
DVD player $350
TV Game $200
Blender $50
Rice Cooker $50
Microwave oven $300
Couch $500
Dining chairs and table $500

KNOXBRAIN 501-55

In Focus: *Amazing Inventions*

What do you think of these inventions: tiny dusters you can put on a cat's feet, so it can clean your floors for you; a hat that holds a roll of tissue for hay-fever sufferers; a sign you can wear on the train so people know where to wake you up to get off? They may sound strange, but they're all real creations. They are examples of the art of *Chindogu*, a Japanese word meaning "odd tool." Chindogu was started by a Japanese journalist, Kenji Kawakami, who has published several books on the subject, including *101 Unuseless Japanese Inventions*. There is even an International Chindogu Society, which has a list of ten tenets, including: "Chindogu are tools for everyday life" and "Humor must not be the only reason for creating a Chindogu." *What do you think of the idea of Chindogu? What other Chindogu ideas can you think of?*

I think there should be seat belts on bicycles to make them safer.

I'd like to see remote controlled microwave ovens, so I could cook from the living room.

How about waterproof business suits, so I wouldn't need an umbrella?

view

Units 1–5

1

 A **Three people are talking about their jobs. Listen and number the pictures (1–3). One picture is extra.**

B **Listen again. Write the words that helped you decide.**

1. _____ 2. _____ 3. _____

2

 A **Listen to the conversation and check (✔) the words you hear.**

- ☐ jealous
- ☑ impatient
- ☑ nervous

- ☐ director
- ☑ producer
- ☐ newscaster

- ☐ engagement
- ☑ birthday
- ☑ anniversary

- ☑ corkscrew
- ☐ kettle
- ☑ spatula

B **Listen again. Note the information you hear about each of Jim's relatives.**

Jim's father

Jim's mother

Jim's brother

Jim's sister

_____ _____ _____ _____

_____ _____ _____ _____

3

A
What is each person complaining about? Listen and number the items (1–4). One is extra.

B
What is wrong with each item? Listen again and write the problem.

1. _____   3. _____
2. _____   4. _____

4

A
Read the statements. Then listen to the conversation and circle *T* for *True*, *F* for *False*, or *U* for *Unknown*.

1. Jim, Jerry, and Joanne know most of the people at the party.   T   F   U
2. Jim's father proposed to his mother in a restroom.   T   F   U
3. Jerry bought his parents' gifts at less than regular price.   T   F   U
4. Jim's father will enjoy the orchestra.   T   F   U
5. Jim's parents are about to make a speech.   T   F   U

B
Listen again and write the gifts they bought.

Jerry:

_____

_____

Joanne:

_____

_____

Jim and Carrie:

_____

_____

5

Listen and circle the answers that are right for you.

1. Yes, I think it's OK.   No, I don't think you should. ✓   It depends on the situation.
2. Something for the kitchen.   Something for the living room.   Something for the bedroom.
3. Yes, several times.   Yes, a few times.   No, I never have.
4. A book or a CD.   An electronic gadget.   A fashion item.

I thought you spoke English!

Goals
- Distinguishing between varieties of English
- Following an academic lecture

1

A Do you know the meaning of these words? Check with a partner, or use a dictionary.

passport	coffee	mosquito	hamburger	cruise
sauna	karate	tea	violin	ketchup

B Look at the map. Write one word from Task A that originally came from each language.

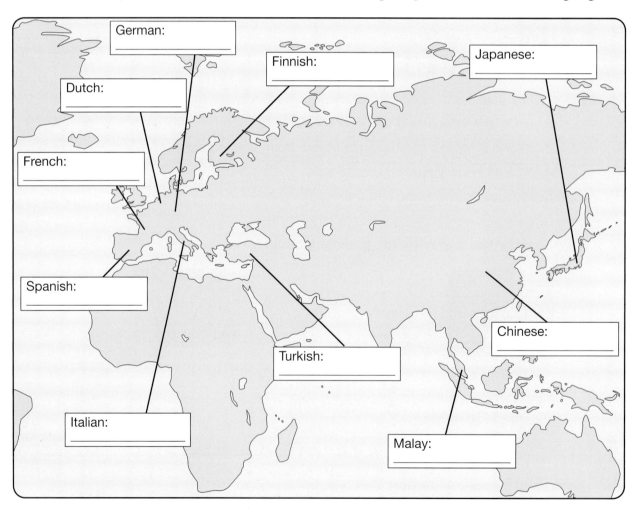

German: _____

Finnish: _____

Japanese: _____

Dutch: _____

French: _____

Spanish: _____

Turkish: _____

Chinese: _____

Italian: _____

Malay: _____

C **Brainstorm!** Work with a partner. Do you know of any words from your language that have been taken into English? Are there any English words that have been taken into your language? Make a list.

2

A Listen to the lecture, and circle the correct answer.

1. This lecture is about . . .
   a. styles of English teaching.
   b. the English language.
   c. learning vocabulary.

2. Different varieties of English . . .
   a. have different vocabularies.
   b. have different spellings and pronunciation.
   c. Both a and b.

B Listen again and check your answers for Task 1B on page 34.

3

A Listen to the conversation and circle *T* for *True*, *F* for *False*, or *U* for *Unknown*.

1. The man is American.	T	F	U
2. The man is staying in this hotel.	T	F	U
3. He is on vacation.	T	F	U
4. The lobby is on the second floor.	T	F	U
5. The man bought some candy.	T	F	U
6. The man is a good driver.	T	F	U

> **Listen for it**
>
> *Sure (do/am/is)!* is an informal way, used mainly in American English, to agree with something someone has said.

B Listen again and circle the British English equivalent for these American words.

American English	British English equivalent	
elevator	lift	escalator
sidewalk	footpath	pavement
rest room	bath	toilet
candy store	sweets shop	off license
first floor	ground floor	second floor
faucet	plug	tap
gas	petrol	kerosene
trunk	boot	bonnet

4

A Listen to the conversation and number the Australian English expressions (1–5) in the order you hear them.

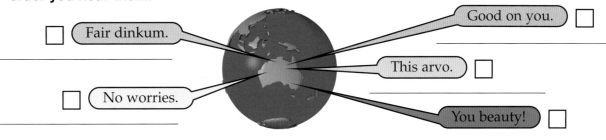

Fair dinkum. ☐

Good on you. ☐

This arvo. ☐

No worries. ☐

You beauty! ☐

B Listen again. What does each phrase mean? Write a short definition for each phrase.

I thought you spoke English!

5

A Listen to the example sentence as spoken by three speakers from different countries.

    1. American   **2.** British   **3.** Australian

B Listen to eight sentences. What type of English do you hear? Write the sentence number(s) under each picture.

American

British

Australian

_____   _____   _____

C Listen again and check your answers. How are the accents different? Discuss with a partner.

6

A Listen to the lecture, and circle the correct answer for each question.

> **Listen for it**
>
> *Now* can be used when you want to get someone's attention.

1. Spanish	English	Chinese
2. 200 million	400 million	600 million
3. fewer	the same	more
4. 65%	80%	95%
5. Thailand	Mexico	Singapore

B Listen again and check your answers. Write any additional information you hear.

_____

7

Listen and circle the answers that are right for you.

1. It's crazy!	It's OK.	It's not as bad as my language.
2. I like it.	It's OK.	I prefer American English.
3. Doesn't everyone?	Sometimes.	Not really.
4. Oh, absolutely.	I'm not sure.	No, not really.
5. Yes, it has.	No, it hasn't.	I don't really understand the difference.

Your Turn! 🔊

Talking about the English language

- What do you think is the best form of English to learn?
  I think **American** English, because it's **the most useful for doing business**.
- Native or non-native speakers—which make the best English teachers?
  Native speakers are better, because they **have the best pronunciation**.
  Non-native speakers, because they **know what it's like to learn English as a foreign language**.
- Do you think a non-native speaker can become fluent in a foreign language?
  I think **it is possible**, but **it would take a long time**.
- Do you think we should all speak the same kind of English?
  My feeling is that there should be **one kind**, so **it will be easier to communicate**.
  It's best if there are **different types**. **It makes communication more interesting**.

Try this . . .

What do you think? Complete the survey and discuss your answers with a partner. Prepare a short talk to support your point of view.

	Agree	Disagree	Not sure
1. American English is the best form of English to learn.			
2. Native English speakers make better English teachers than non-native speakers.			
3. There is no such thing as "correct" English.			
4. It is impossible to become completely fluent in a foreign language.			
5. There should be one form of English that everyone speaks.			

In Focus: *Crazy spelling*

One of the problems in learning to read and write English is that there is a complicated relationship between the sounds of the language and the letters of the alphabet that represent those sounds. The writer George Bernard Shaw once pointed out that the word "fish" could also be spelled "ghoti." "Gh" has the same sound as "f" in words such as "enough," "tough," and "cough." In the word "women," the "o" is pronounced as an "i." And in "nation," "ti" is pronounced as "sh." American English has generally attempted to simplify the spelling system—for example, by leaving off unnecessary or unpronounced letters. So, the word that is spelled "programme" in British English is spelled "program" in American English; "dialogue" is spelled "dialog." *How would you change English to make it easier to learn?*

English has too many words. I'd reduce the number of words.

I'd create one standard international English that everyone around the world would speak.

I'd make the spelling of English phonetic. Words should be spelt how they sound.

You'll buy anything.

Goals
- Understanding ad messages
- Recognizing approval and disapproval

1

A What is each advertisement for? Use the words in the box to label each ad.

cordless headphones	key finder	stair exerciser	inflatable bed
electric clippers	electric peeler	shower radio	talking bathroom scale

Makes hard work a thing of the past.

Uses new Ultra-Titanium technology!

Walk your way to a slimmer, fitter body.

As used by top TV stars!

Enjoy music and privacy anywhere.

Made in America, by Americans!

Tells you your *exact* weight.

99.99% accuracy guaranteed!

Perfect for overnight guests, or for camping.

As comfortable as sleeping in a luxury hotel!

YOU'LL NEVER LOSE YOUR KEYS AGAIN.

The new gadget everybody wants!

Add music to your morning.

Be the first in your neighborhood to get one!

Cutting hair was never so easy.

No more embarrassing neck hair!

B Which product would you buy? Why? Discuss with a partner.

C **Brainstorm!** Work with a partner. Make a list of ads you've seen recently. What ads do you like, and why? What ads don't you like, and why?

2

A Listen to four advertisements. Which of the products in Task 1A are they advertising? Write the type of product for each ad.

Product	Key words
1.	
2.	
3.	
4.	

B Listen again and write the key words that helped you decide.

3

A Listen to Joe and his wife, Kimberley, talking about Joe's purchases. What items did Joe buy, and why?

Listen for it

Like what? is an informal way to ask someone to give more specific examples.

Joe bought	Why?	Does Kimberley approve?
_____	_____	yes no
_____	_____	yes no
_____	_____	yes no
_____	_____	yes no

B Listen again. Does Kimberley approve of each purchase? Circle *yes* or *no*.

4

A In rapid speech, a *t* at the end of a word, before and after a consonant sound, is sometimes left off. Listen to the example sentence.

Example: We really don'~~t~~ need it.

B Look at the following sentences. Predict where you think that the *t* sound might be left off. Listen and check your answers.

1. I won't have to go to the barber anymore.

2. I wouldn't say that.

3. That doesn't look very strong.

4. I must get one of those gadgets.

5. It's the newest car on the market.

6. I can just listen to my own singing.

C Listen again. Practice saying these sentences with a partner.

5

A **Listen to the lecture on advertising techniques. Number the techniques in the order the lecturer talks about them.**

Listen for it

People often say *In fact* when they are about to add more information.

Technique	Definition
____ The bandwagon	• a famous person uses the product
____ Facts and figures	• using the product will make you live like rich and famous people
____ Magic ingredients	• this product will protect you from danger
____ Snob appeal	• using numbers to impress the consumer
____ Avant-garde	• a special ingredient or technology makes the product work
____ Patriotism	• use the product to be like everyone else
____ Testimonial	• using this will put you ahead of everyone else
____ Hidden fears	• using this product shows you love your country

B **Listen again and match each technique to its definition.**

C **Work with a partner. Look again at the advertisements in Task 1. Which technique is used in each one?**

cordless headphones: _____   electric clippers: _____

key finder: _____   electric peeler: _____

stair exerciser: _____   shower radio: _____

inflatable bed: _____   talking bathroom scale: _____

6

Listen and circle the answers that are right for you.

1. No, I don't need one.   That would really save time.
2. I could do with one of those.   I never lose them anyway.
3. That sounds great.   But I don't cook.
4. I don't have many visitors.   That would be useful.
5. I wouldn't waste my money on that.   That might be good to have.

Your Turn! 🔊

Convincing customers to buy a product

- The great thing is **it's so easy to use**.
- It's **definitely for you**.
- Available now **for a limited time**.
- **Losing weight** has never been so **easy**, or **so fun**.
- If you **love music**, you're going to **love Freesound**.
- Available at **any of our stores**.
- It'll really **save you money**.
- If you call now you'll get **these great knives as a special gift**.

Try this . . .

Work in groups. Choose a product and make a radio ad. Try to convince other groups to buy the product. Think about the questions on the right.

What's the product?

_____

_____

_____

Who is the target market?

_____

_____

_____

Why should they buy it?

_____

_____

_____

_____

What selling techniques will you use?

_____

_____

_____

_____

In Focus: *Buy Nothing Day*

Do you go shopping every day? Imagine a day when you didn't buy anything. Now imagine a day when *no one* bought anything. This is the dream of the organizers of "International Buy Nothing Day." The point of the day is that for 24 hours, on the last Friday in November, no one should buy anything. Buy Nothing Day was started in 1991 by a Canadian activist, in a protest against consumerism and waste, and has grown to be celebrated in dozens of countries, by thousands of people. To celebrate the day, one store in Ottawa, Canada, placed an "International Buy Nothing Day" poster in the window and the employees had a paid holiday. The year after that, they opened the shop and served cookies and coffee to the customers, but refused to make a sale. *What do you think of the idea of Buy Nothing Day? Could you go a day without buying anything?*

I think it's a waste of time. People should be allowed to shop if they want.

I really support the idea. There's just too much focus on materialism in our society.

I love shopping! But I don't see a problem with having one day off.

UNIT 8

Our sales target is $1.1 million.

Goals
- Identifying large numbers
- Understanding business data

1

A Match the expressions on the left of each column with the numbers on the right.

1. 5.5 million • • 55,000,000
2. 550 thousand • • 5,500
3. 55K • • 55,000
4. 55 hundred • • 5,500,000
5. 55m • • 550,000

6. three grand • • 300,000
7. 300K • • 36
8. three mil • • 30,000
9. thirty Gs • • 3,000
10. three dozen • • 3,000,000

B Use the information on the pieces of paper to complete the company balance sheet.

Inventory
$210 thousand

Total liabilities 1.05 mil

A/R total
$585K

Expenses

| Date | Item | Purpose | Amount |

$200 grand
for A/P

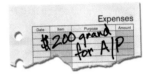

Bldg.
depreciation
0.11m

Balance Sheet						January 1, 2003

Newman Industries Inc.

Assets			Claims on Assets		
Current Assets			Current Liabilities		
Cash	$145,000		Accounts Payable		
Marketable Securities	$215,000		Notes Payable	$250,000	
Accounts Receivable			Total Current Liabilities	$450,000	
Inventories					
Total Current Assets		$1,155,000	Long-Term Note	$600,000	
			Total Liabilities		
Long Term Assets			Owner's Equity		$1,750,000
Building (Gross)	$1,160,000				
(Accumulated Depreciation)			**Total Claims**		**$2,800,000**
Building (Net)	$1,050,000				
Land	$595,000				
Total Long Term Assets		$1,645,000			
Total Assets		**$2,800,000**			

C Brainstorm! Make a list of five big companies in your country. What do you know about them? Discuss with a partner.

2

A Listen to the news stories and number the headlines (1–6) in the correct order.

Lost climbers last seen around _____ meters

Yasuhara Comet passes _____ miles from Earth

Population of more Asian cities to pass _____ by 2010

Student who wins _____ won't quit

Big Kevin scores big deal in _____ contract signing

The Sunday Times
_____ turn out for concert

B Listen again and complete the headlines with the correct numbers.

3

A Listen to the sales meeting and continue the graph for Michael's sales for April to June.

Listen for it

At the last minute means at the last possible time, for example, just before a deadline.

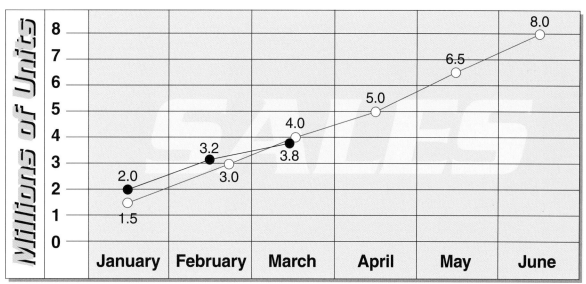

Millions of Units

	January	February	March	April	May	June

Actual: 2.0, 3.2, 3.8
Planned: 1.5, 3.0, 4.0, 5.0, 6.5, 8.0

—○— Planned
—●— Actual

B Listen again. Write the reasons why Michael didn't make his sales goals.

Month	Reason
April	
May	
June	

Our sales target is $1.1 million.

4

A In spoken English, extra sounds are sometimes inserted between words in a process known as intrusion. Listen to the example.

Example: I've been working here for three-and-a-half years. (no *y* intrusion)
I've been working here for three-*y*and-a-half years. (*y* intrusion)

B Look at these sentences and predict where you might hear a *y* intrusion. Now listen and check. Practice saying the sentences to a partner.

1. He even said he won't be able to make the meeting.

2. The president said the economy is growing at about eight percent.

3. Apart from me and Tom, three other people are working on the project.

4. I think you'll agree America is more powerful economically than ever.

5

A Listen to the sales meetings and number the sales graphs (1–3).

> **Listen for it**
>
> *So far* is used to mean *until now; that's not so far off* means *that's almost right.*

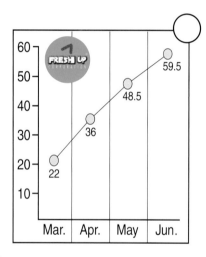 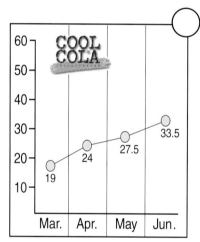 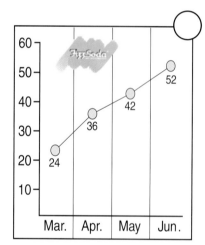

B Look at these extracts from the conversations. Listen again and write in the missing verbs.

1. . . . we only _____ 3,500,000 in sales . . .

2. . . . in June, we _____ 6,000,000 . . .

3. . . . we only _____ 12,500,000 in May.

4. . . . in June, we _____ only 11,000,000.

5. . . . an increase of 12,000,000 _____ us to a total of 36,000,000 . . .

6. . . . in June, we _____ an increase of 10,000,000 . . .

6

Listen and circle the answers that are right for you.

1. Yes, very good.   It's not bad.   Not really.

2. Sure, why not?   I doubt it.   No way.

3. Absolutely.   I'm not sure.   I'd need more.

Your Turn!

Talking about charity donations

- I'd probably give **half of it** to the **Anti-Landmine Foundation**.
  I don't think that would be a good use of the money.
- Let's give **300 thousand** to **The Cancer Society**.
  That's a good idea. **Cancer's something that can affect anyone.**
  I think it's a waste of money. **We'll never find a cure.**
- I think **the Endangered Wildlife Fund** deserves the most.
  I don't care much about **wildlife**. I'm more concerned about **starving children.**
- How about we **divide it equally between three of the groups**?
  No, why don't we **give some money to each group**?
  I'd rather donate **everything to Education for the Poor**.

Try this . . .

Work with a partner. You and your partner work on the charity committee of a big international company. You have $100 million to divide among various charities. Discuss and decide how you will divide the money. Give a reason for your decisions.

Charity	Amount	Reason
The Cancer Society		
Endangered Wildlife Fund		
Anti-Landmine Foundation		
Help the Starving Children		
Education for the Poor		
Other . . .		

In Focus: *America's richest give something back*

For many years *Forbes* magazine has published an annual list of the 400 richest individuals in the United States. In 1996 Ted Turner, one of the individuals on the list, criticized the list for encouraging greed, and suggested that someone compile a list of the people who gave away the most money. Turner, who pledged 1 billion dollars to the United Nations, wanted to encourage the rich to give more of their wealth away. Since 1996, *Slate*, an online magazine, has compiled an annual list of the 60 biggest philanthropists in America. The list for 2001 showed that these 60 people (or couples) gave away, or promised to give away, a total of almost 13 billion dollars. Bill Gates and his wife have frequently been at the top of the list, and in 2001, they gave away or pledged 2 billion dollars. Still, even that was only good enough for the number two spot. The number one donor for that year was Andrew Grove, founder of Intel, and his wife, who gave away a total of over 6 billion dollars. *Do you think a list like this one helps to encourage generosity? Do you think these people give away enough money?*

I think those millionaires can afford to give away more. I don't think they're generous enough.

I'd rather see them pay more taxes than give money away. That way more people would benefit.

I really think they're doing a good thing. They should be congratulated.

Our sales target is $1.1 million.

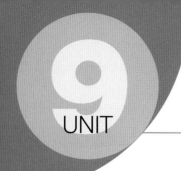

UNIT 9

I have a driving lesson tonight.

Goals | • Understanding sequence of events
• Identifying information on the telephone

1

A What are these vehicles? Use the words below to label the pictures.

(dump truck)   (18-wheeler)   (tractor)   (bulldozer)

(forklift)   (cement mixer)   (scooter)

_____   _____   _____   _____

_____   _____   _____

B Match the verbs with the prepositions to make phrasal verbs. Each word may be used more than once.

(start) (turn) (back) (drive) (back) (pull) (run) (lift) (set)

(on) (up) (in) (out) (over) (into) (across) (down) (off)

_____

_____

_____

C **Brainstorm!** Work with a partner. Which of the phrasal verbs above relate to driving? Discuss with your partner.

A Listen to Shirley talking to five people. What is the purpose of each conversation?

1. **Shirley is calling to . . .**
   a. get some information.
   b. give some information.
   c. confirm some information.

2. **She wants to . . .**
   a. make an appointment.
   b. change an appointment.
   c. confirm an appointment.

3. **She has called to . . .**
   a. cancel her lesson.
   b. reschedule her lesson.
   c. confirm her lesson.

4. **She has called to . . .**
   a. make an appointment
   b. cancel her lesson.
   c. confirm her lesson.

5. **She has decided to . . .**
   a. cancel her lesson.
   b. reschedule her lesson.
   c. take two lessons.

B Listen again and check your answers. When is Shirley's appointment? _____

A Number the pictures (1–4) in the order in which you think they happened. Then, listen and check your answers.

Listen for it

Don't tell me is used informally, usually in amusement or surprise, to indicate you know what a person plans to say next.

B Listen again and circle the expressions you hear. (Note: the form of the verb may be different.) Then, using the expressions below, tell Shirley's story to a partner.

drive back	drive up	start out	start up	pull in	pull over
back into	back up	back out	run over	run into	run up onto

I have a driving lesson tonight.

4

A **Listen to the dialog and check (✔) the vehicle the people are talking about.**

Listen for it

Whatchamacallit is an informal way of identifying something you can't remember the name of.

B **Listen again. What instructions does the man get? Check (✔) the instructions you hear.**

Do . . .

☐ honk before backing up.

☐ use the lights when reversing.

☐ release the parking brake before driving.

☐ honk while turning.

☐ keep the load 8 inches off the ground.

Don't . . .

☐ drive faster than 5 mph.

☐ park the vehicle on a hill.

☐ lift more than 4,000 pounds.

☐ tilt the load while driving.

☐ leave the keys in the vehicle.

5

A **Expressions such as *um*, *uh*, and *let's see* are known as fillers as they are used to fill pauses in sentences or conversations. Listen to the example.**

> **Example:** (with fillers) Let's see, let me, uh, show you, um, what you'll be doing.
> (without fillers) Let me show you what you'll be doing.

B **Listen and write the sentences you hear *without* the fillers.**

1. _____   4. _____

2. _____   5. _____

3. _____   6. _____

C **Listen again and practice saying the sentences, with and without using fillers.**

6

Listen and circle the answers that are right for you.

1. Almost every day.   Sometimes.   Never.

2. Sure, no problem.   I could try.   I don't think so.

3. Yes, it does.   I'm not sure.   It's not too bad.

4. Yes, it's pretty heavy.   It's about average.   No, it's pretty light.

Your Turn! 🔊

Asking and talking about transportation

- Which types of transportation do you use most often?
  I **take the subway to work** every day and I sometimes **take the bus** on weekends.
  I **drive** almost every day.
- If you could have any type of car, which one would you choose?
  I'd definitely want **a Porsche** because **it's one of the fastest cars in the world**.
  I'd probably get **an SUV**. I like **their size**.
- Do you think you can tell someone's personality by the car they drive?
  Yeah, I think people who drive **sedans** are **conservative** and **sports car** drivers are more **liberal**.
  No, not really. **Personality is deeper than that**.
- What do you see as the city's biggest transportation problem?
  Traffic jams are a problem, but even worse is **the overcrowding on subways**.

Try this . . .

Ask a partner the questions on the right. Add a question of your own. Ask follow-up questions to find out more information.

Transportation Survey | **Details**

1. Which types of transportation do you use most often? _____
2. Which type of motor vehicle would you like to own? _____
3. Do you think a car says something about its driver? _____
4. What's your city's biggest transportation problem? _____
5. How could transportation in your city be improved? _____
6. _____ ? _____

In Focus: *The difference engine*

One of the greatest transport innovators was famed American architect and designer Richard Buckminster Fuller, the brains behind the groundbreaking Dymaxion car. Introduced in 1933, the Dymaxion was 20 feet long and capable of carrying eleven passengers comfortably, despite weighing about as much as a VW Beetle. Made of aluminum to prevent rust, the Dymaxion's revolutionary features included the world's first car air-conditioner, shatterproof glass, a rear engine, and front-wheel drive. It was also intended to fly, once suitable materials became available. Although the Dymaxion never caught on the way Fuller had hoped, it inspired many others who dared to imagine new and improved modes of human transportation. *In what ways do you think the cars of today could be improved? What future changes do you foresee in the kinds of transportation that people use?*

I'd like to see a car that runs on water and doesn't pollute the air.

Someday we'll probably all travel around in flying cars.

I think cars will be obsolete in 20 years and we'll all use jet packs.

I have a driving lesson tonight.

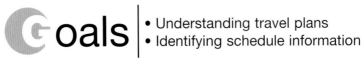

She wants a seat to Miami.

Goals
- Understanding travel plans
- Identifying schedule information

1

A Look at the messages from a secretary to a travel agent. Use the information to complete the travel form. Then compare answers with a partner.

12/03 Tues 09:55 FAX 555-4571 ADAIR ENTERPRISES

Adair Enterprises   March 12
84 River Way, Singapore 192118   Attn: Nick Chua
tel: 555-4271   Reservations Manager
fax: 555-4571   All Seasons Travel
www.adairenterprises.com   44 East Bridge St.
                                                  #03-15, Singapore 192404

Nick,
Thanks for the flight schedules you sent over. Here's what I need:

Please reserve a one-way ticket to New York for Ms. Elizabeth Tan on All Asia flight 4157 at 2:50 p.m. on March 19 and a ticket on MidWest Air flight 368 from New York to Chicago on March 23 at 6:35 a.m. You can book MidWest again for the trip from Chicago to L.A. at 2:25 that afternoon. The flight number is MW455.

It looks like Pacifica Airlines has the only flight from L.A. to Singapore without a stopover, so please book a seat on PA549 on March 26 at 5:40 a.m.

All tickets are business class and Ms. Tan prefers a window seat. As always, please bill us for the cost of the flights.

Thanks for all your help,
Pat

Date: 14 Mar. Time: 4:43 pm
For: Nick
While you were out...
Name: Pat Lim
Tel: 555-4272 ☑ Urgent
Message:
Forgot to mention Ms. Tan is vegetarian. Also her AA frequent flyer number is 027-45138.

Reservation Application

Passenger's Name: _____

Company: _____

Frequent Flyer ☐ Yes ☐ No Airline: _____ Number: _____

Destination: _____ Date: _____ Flight No.: _____ Departure time: _____

(1) _____

(2) _____

(3) _____

(4) _____

Class: First / Executive / Economy

Special Requirements: _____

Payment: Cash / Credit Card / Billing

B **Brainstorm!** Work with a partner. Can you think of any other travel-related vocabulary? Add to the list.

arrival, departure, aisle seat, . . .

2

A **Listen to the conversations and number the pictures (1–3).**

Listen for it

If something *doesn't mattter*, it means it is not important.

B **Listen again. Why is Pat calling? Circle the purpose of each conversation.**

1. make a reservation
   reconfirm a reservation

2. cancel a reservation
   change a reservation

3. reconfirm a flight
   cancel a flight

3

A **When and why does Pat's boss want to go to each of the following places? Listen again and write the arrival date and reason in the spaces below.**

Miami   Chicago   Los Angeles   Singapore

Date: _____   Date: _____   Date: _____   Date: _____

Reason: _____   Reason: _____   Reason: _____   Reason: _____

B **Listen again and check your answers.**

4

A **Look at the two example sentences, and listen to the two different pronunciations of the word *you*. In Example 1, *you* is unstressed, and is known as a weak form.**

Example 1: What would you like?   **Example 2:** I'm not invited, but you are.

B **Listen to the following sentences and underline the weak forms that you hear. Then listen again and check your answers. Practice saying these sentences with a partner.**

1. Are you waiting for a flight?

2. I'm leaving for Seoul at ten.

3. Are you thinking of flying business class?

4. I'm flying from Miami to Seoul.

5. The flight leaves at once for Miami.

She wants a seat to Miami.

5

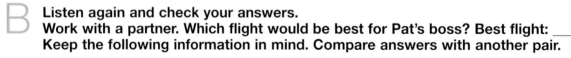

A **Listen and complete the airline schedule.**

Pacific Tours
Your Travel Partner

	Flight	Time	Airport	Availability
1	All Asia AA0890	8:00 a.m. _____	Changi Int'l (Singapore) Narita Int'l (Tokyo)	1st Class, Economy
	All Asia _____	6:30 p.m. _____	Narita Int'l (Tokyo) San Francisco Int'l	1st Class, Business, Economy
	East Coast _____	1:30 p.m. _____	San Francisco Int'l Miami Int'l	1st Class, Business, Economy
2	All Asia _____	7:00 a.m. _____	Changi Int'l (Singapore) San Francisco Int'l	1st Class, Business, Economy
	East Coast _____	_____ 10:30 p.m.	San Francisco Int'l Miami Int'l	1st Class, Business, Economy
3	All Asia AA0881	_____ 12:55 p.m.	Changi Int'l (Singapore) Los Angeles Int'l	1st Class, Economy
	East Coast _____	4:10 p.m. _____	Los Angeles Int'l Miami Int'l	1st Class, Business, Economy

B **Listen again and check your answers.**
Work with a partner. Which flight would be best for Pat's boss? Best flight: _____
Keep the following information in mind. Compare answers with another pair.

- She wants to travel business class.
- She wants the least number of stops.
- She wants to arrive in Miami in the early evening.

6

Listen and circle the answers that are right for you.

1.	Yes, many times.	A few times.	No, I haven't.
2.	I love it.	It's OK.	No, not really.
3.	Plane.	Train.	I don't really use either.
4.	No, not at all.	Sometimes.	It terrifies me.
5.	Yes, I really do.	Sometimes.	No, not at all.

Your Turn!

Making travel arrangements

- Could I **make a reservation**, please?
- May I **have your departure date**?
- I'm sorry but **there are no seats available on that date**.
- Is that **a one-way or round-trip ticket**?
- Would you prefer **first, business, or economy class**?
- Would you like **a window or an aisle seat**?
- Will that be **cash or credit card**?

Try this . . .

Student A You want to travel from Singapore to Miami. Ask your partner for your travel options and note the information. Do not look at the schedule in Task 4. Choose one of the options and say why.

Student B You are a travel agent. Your partner wants to travel from Singapore to Miami. Look at the schedule in Task 4 and explain your partner's options.

In Focus: *Safety in the air*

Following the aircraft hijackings of September 11th, 2001, airlines around the world have been faced with the same problems—how to improve security on planes without inconveniencing passengers too much. Suggestions to improve security include: tighter check-in security and matching bags to passengers before boarding; banning hand luggage completely; making bombproof cargo holds; making the cockpit doors bulletproof; using an automatic guidance system to fly and land a hijacked plane, from the ground; using video surveillance on planes; and using air marshals (armed sky police, disguised as passengers) to sit on each flight. Some of these ideas are practical, and are used now, while others are too expensive, or would be too difficult to implement. *What do you think of these suggestions? Which of them do you think would work? Can you think of any others?*

> I don't mind experiencing more inconvenience, if it means traveling becomes safer.

> I think the whole situation is over-emphasized. People don't need to worry so much.

> I don't think hand luggage should be banned—that's going too far.

She wants a seat to Miami. 53

Oview

Units 6–10

1

A Three people are giving talks at a meeting of Global Multimedia Inc. Listen and match each territory with the correct chart. One chart is extra.

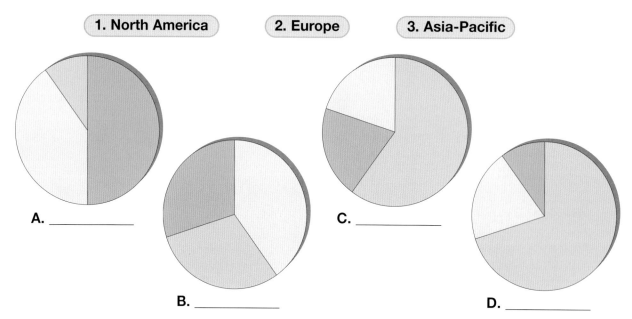

1. North America   2. Europe   3. Asia-Pacific

A. _____

B. _____

C. _____

D. _____

B Listen again and label the parts of each chart with the correct division (N = Newspapers, T = Television, C = Computer software).

What was each territory's total revenue?

North America: US$ _____   Europe: US$ _____   Asia-Pacific: US$ _____

2

A Listen to the conversation and fill in the flight schedules.

Date	Flight	From	Departure	To	Arrival
July 19	EC		7:00 a.m.	Los Angeles	
	AA	Los Angeles			6:15 p.m. (+1)
July 21	EC 458		9:00 a.m.		12:00 p.m.
	AA	San Francisco		Bangkok	

B Listen again and check your answers.

Which flight will they take? _____ Why? _____

54

3

A Read the statements. Then listen to the conversation and circle *T* for *True*, *F* for *False*, and *U* for *Unknown*.

1. It was raining hard.	T	F	U
2. Jim didn't see the tractor pull out.	T	F	U
3. Jim used his brakes too late.	T	F	U
4. The tractor was badly damaged.	T	F	U
5. Jim had to walk home.	T	F	U
6. Jim's car is being repaired.	T	F	U

B Listen again to check your answers.
What kind of car do they want to buy? _____

4

A Listen to ads for three different cars. Note the features special to each one, and the price.

Diablo

Features: _____
_____

Price: _____

Venus

Features: _____
_____

Price: _____

Electra

Features: _____
_____

Price: _____

B Listen again and check your answers. Which car do you think would be most suitable for the couple in Task 3? Discuss with a partner.

Car: _____ Reason(s): _____

5

Listen and circle the answers that are right for you.

1. American English.	British English.	Australian English.
2. TV ads.	Newspaper ads.	Radio ads.
3. Yes, many times.	Yes, but not often.	No, I never have.
4. Speed.	Safety.	Size.
5. A long time ago.	Recently.	I never have.

How do I get downtown?

Goals
- Understanding directions
- Understanding telephone conversations

1

A **Look at the map and read the directions. Where is each person giving directions to? Fill in the blanks.**

1 Go down Stockton Street for two blocks and turn right into Market Street. _____ is on your left.

2 Go along Post Street to Market Street and turn left. Go straight right to the end. _____ is in front of you, across the road.

3 Go up Stockton Street to Pine Street and turn right, then go along Pine Street past Kearny Street. _____ is on your left.

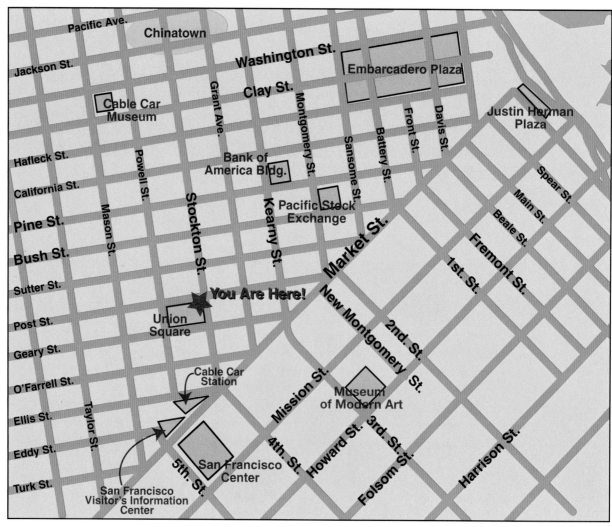

B **Brainstorm! Work with a partner. Make a list of places of interest in your local area. Practice giving directions from a central location.**

A Listen and number the pictures (1–3). One picture is extra.

B Listen again and circle the best answer.

1. How long is it from the airport to downtown San Francisco?
   (**a**) 14 minutes   (**b**) 40 minutes   (**c**) 45 minutes

2. What does Hideki find out in the arrival area?
   (**a**) how to get downtown   (**b**) which shuttle to take   (**c**) where the shuttles are

3. Where is Hideki planning to stay?
   (**a**) the Bayside Hotel   (**b**) the Union Hotel   (**c**) the Downtown Hotel

4. What information does Hideki get from Ed?
   (**a**) directions to the shuttle bus stop   (**c**) directions to the rental car counter
   (**b**) directions to the information counter

A Listen to the dialog and circle the names of the locations you hear.

> ## Listen for it
>
> *Check* is an informal way of expressing understanding or stating that a task is done.

gift shop	fitness center
front office	conference rooms
elevators	guest rooms
lounge	restaurant
business center	lobby

B Listen again. Where does Erik advise Hideki to go? Label the three places on the map.

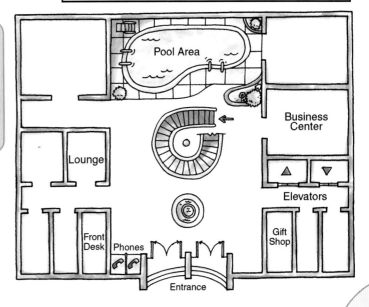

4

A In spoken English, when a word ending in a consonant sound precedes a word starting with a vowel, the two are usually linked. Look at the example.

> **Example:**   Are there any shops in the hotel?   Are there any shops in the hotel?

B Listen and draw lines between the words that are linked by the speakers. Then listen again and practice.

1. Do you have an umbrella I could borrow?
2. What time are we supposed to come up to the office tomorrow?
3. Have you made any long-distance phone calls since you arrived?

4. I'll make a reservation for five in the hotel restaurant.
5. Hideki and Erik are at Underwater World until five.
6. I gave Anne my camera and briefcase at the office yesterday.

5

A Hideki is asking a hotel concierge for directions in downtown San Francisco. Listen and draw a line on page 56 to trace his planned route through the area.

B Listen again and check your answers.

> **Listen for it**
>
> *You can't miss it* is used informally when giving directions to suggest that a location is easy to find.

6

Listen and circle the answers that are right for you.

1. Yeah, it's pretty far.   It's not too far.   No, it's not far at all.
2. By subway.   By taxi.   By bus.
3. Yes, a lot.   Some.   None at all.
4. Yes, very good.   I'm not bad.   No, not really.
5. All the time.   Yeah, sometimes.   No, not often.
6. Sure, no problem.   I guess so.   I don't think so.

Your Turn! 🔊

Asking about locations and giving directions

- Could you recommend a good place to eat?
  Sure, **Carmichael's Seafood** is nearby.
- What's the best way to get there?
- How would I get there?
  Go up Dundas St to Richmond and **turn left**.
- Do you know a good park around here?
  Sure, **City Park** is **just past the museum, on your left.**
- Is there **a car rental agency** nearby?
  There's one on **8th Ave and Cline St.**
  Take the **next left**, and you'll see it **on your right.**
- Is there a **gallery** around here?
  Yeah, there's one **about two streets down on your right.**

Try this . . .

Work with a partner. Think of three things you'd like to do tonight. Ask your partner to recommend some places and give you directions. Take notes.

In Focus: *Eye in the sky*

From helping the military keep track of its forces, to helping commuters find the best way home, the Global Positioning System (GPS) is such a widely used technology that it's easy to forget it's relatively new. Dating from the late 1970s and early '80s, the GPS is a set of 24 satellites that orbit the earth and make it possible to pinpoint the exact location of everything from tanks and aircraft to cars and even pets. From anywhere on earth, portable GPS units can be used to receive satellite data on the receiver's latitude, longitude, altitude, and speed of travel. Though used primarily to track delivery vehicles and shipments, GPS technology has also been used to keep tabs on criminal parolees, catch speeding rental car users, and locate emergency 911 callers. *How do you feel about the use of GPS for these purposes? What are some other possible uses of GPS technology? Can you see any potential for misuse?*

It's fine to track criminals but is it really necessary to monitor ordinary people?

I think GPS could be really useful for finding lost children and runaways.

I'm worried GPS could be used to watch people, like in the book *1984*.

UNIT

Is this where I get my student ID?

oals | • Identifying purpose
| • Following a sequence of events

1

A What's important in deciding on which university to attend? Complete the survey below.

University Survey

Use the scale to rate how important each item is to you.

		Not Important ←				→ Very Important	
1	Number of students	0	1	2	3	4	5
2	Official ranking	0	1	2	3	4	5
3	Reputation	0	1	2	3	4	5
4	Location	0	1	2	3	4	5
5	Courses offered	0	1	2	3	4	5
6	Admission requirements	0	1	2	3	4	5
7	Facilities	0	1	2	3	4	5
8	Quality of professors	0	1	2	3	4	5
9	Sports / athletic teams	0	1	2	3	4	5
10	Organizations / clubs	0	1	2	3	4	5
11	Tuition costs	0	1	2	3	4	5
12	Scholarship availability	0	1	2	3	4	5

B Work with a partner. Choose a university you know. What do you know about it? Which of the above factors is it well known for?

C **Brainstorm!** Work with a partner. Look at the map on the next page. Where would you go to do the following things?

get a student card	photocopy articles	borrow books	register for classes
pay your tuition fee	work out	get a check up	buy textbooks

2

A **Listen and number the places on the map in the order in which Daniel plans to visit them (1–5).**

B **Listen again. What does Daniel want to do at each place?**

Place	What does he want to do there?
1	
2	
3	
4	
5	

3

A **Daniel is talking to three people. What does he want to do in each conversation?**

Listen for it

I'm afraid so is a polite way of confirming some bad news.

Daniel wants to . . .	Daniel needs to . . .
1.	
2.	
3.	

B **Listen again. Why isn't Daniel able to do what he wants? What does he need to do first?**

Is this where I get my student ID? **61**

4

A Daniel is explaining why he couldn't meet Melanie. Listen and write letters (a–g) on the map to show where he went.

B Listen again and check your answers.

5

A Listen to the example, then listen and circle the sentence in each pair that you hear.

> **Example:**   No, I have two.   No, I have to.

1. Yeah, he has two.   Yeah, he has to.
2. She told me she used two.   She told me she used to.
3. I think they have two.   I think they have to.
4. That's right. She has two.   That's right. She has to.
5. I'm pretty sure he used two.   I'm pretty sure he used to.

B Listen again and check your answers. Practice with a partner.

6

Listen and circle the answers that are right for you.

1. Yes, it does.	Kind of a lot.	No, not that much.
2. Very important.	Reasonably important.	Not very important.
3. Sure, why not?	I'd think about it.	Absolutely not.
4. Yes, I'd say so.	It depends.	No, not really.
5. Definitely.	I'm not sure.	Not particularly.
6. Yeah, it's possible.	It's not likely.	It's almost impossible.

Your Turn! 🔊

Talking about universities

- To save money, we should **get rid of the computer lab.**
  I think so too. **Students can use their laptops instead.**
  I don't agree. **What about students who don't have a computer?**
- I think we should **cut the student cafeteria.**
  I agree, **students could bring their own lunch to university.**
  No, **the cafeteria is a great place to meet and talk.**
- How about **cutting the size of the campus grounds?**
  Yeah, **by selling the park areas for development, we could make a lot of money.**
  I don't think so. **Who wants an ugly university, surrounded by concrete?**

☐ Student cafeteria

☐ Gym/fitness center

☐ Computer lab

☐ Faculty of medicine

☐ Faculty of music

☐ Library

☐ Auditorium/concert hall

☐ Campus medical center

☐ Campus open space

Try this . . .

Work in a small group. You and your partners are members of the funding committee for a university. Unfortunately, your university is in serious financial trouble, and you need to get rid of a number of areas of the university. Look at the list above, and together decide four areas you would remove. Give reasons for your decisions.

In Focus: *The Mozart effect*

Schools in the United States and elsewhere have been embroiled in a controversy in recent years over whether subjects like music and visual arts should be among those on the standard curricula. For millennia, a thorough knowledge of music and art was considered a necessity for anyone who wanted to be truly educated. The feeling was that "art for art's sake" was sufficient justification for studying the finer things in life. But more recently, many societies have begun to question the value of investing in the arts. On one side of the debate are those who cite evidence that students involved in the arts actually score better in more academic subjects like math and science. At the other extreme are those who see the arts as a non-essential part of a core education since they don't address the needs of business and job training. *How important do you think an arts education is for students in your country? Should the primary goal of education be to turn out well-rounded citizens or to give students the essential skills they need to get good jobs?*

I think students need to grow up with an appreciation of art and culture.

When I was in school, I thought music and art were a waste of time and I still do.

The first priority of schools is to produce students who can think for themselves.

It's a really cool site.

Goals | • Understanding opinions
| • Identifying frequency

1

A Read the survey and check the answers that are true for you.

Are you an Internet Addict?

No, not at all ←——————→ Yes, a lot
    1   2   3   4   5

1 ☐ ☐ ☐ ☐ ☐   Do you get excited thinking about going online?

2 ☐ ☐ ☐ ☐ ☐   Do you often spend longer online than you had planned?

3 ☐ ☐ ☐ ☐ ☐   Has your time on the Internet gradually increased?

4 ☐ ☐ ☐ ☐ ☐   Have you ever tried to limit your time online, but failed?

5 ☐ ☐ ☐ ☐ ☐   Do you ever feel guilty about being online?

6 ☐ ☐ ☐ ☐ ☐   Does being online help you forget about your real life?

7 ☐ ☐ ☐ ☐ ☐   Do you think about the Internet when you are not online?

8 ☐ ☐ ☐ ☐ ☐   Has your real life suffered because of the Internet?

9 ☐ ☐ ☐ ☐ ☐   Would it disturb you if you weren't able to get online?

10 ☐ ☐ ☐ ☐ ☐   Do you try to keep the amount of time you spend online a secret?

B Count up your score, and see if you are an Internet addict. Share your answers and score with a partner.

10–20:	You have no problem with the Internet.
21–35:	You may like using the Internet, but you're not yet an addict.
36–50:	You really use the Internet a lot. Remember to spend time in the real world!

C **Brainstorm!** Work with a partner. What uses of the Internet can you think of? Make a list. Rank them according to how important they are to you (1 = most important).

2

🔊 **A** Listen to the conversations. Which ones are about using the Internet? Circle the correct column.

About the Internet? **Key words**

1. yes no unknown _____

2. yes no unknown _____

3. yes no unknown _____

4. yes no unknown _____

5. yes no unknown _____

B Listen again. What key words helped you decide?

3

🔊 **A** Listen to Yuko and George talking about the Internet. What do they use the Internet for? Check (✔) the correct columns.

> **Listen for it**
>
> If you *can't do without* something, it means it's very important for you.

Activity	Yuko		George	
	Yes?	Time	Yes?	Time
Surfing the Web	☐	_____	☐	_____
Getting news, sports, weather	☐	_____	☐	_____
Shopping	☐	_____	☐	_____
Making reservations	☐	_____	☐	_____
Study	☐	_____	☐	_____
Business	☐	_____	☐	_____
Work	☐	_____	☐	_____
Communicating with people	☐	_____	☐	_____

B Listen again. How much time do they spend on each activity?

4

🔊 **A** Brian, George, and Yuko are discussing the pros and cons of using the Internet. Listen and complete the chart.

	Pros	Cons
Brian		
George		
Yuko		

B Listen again and check your answers. Do you agree with them? Discuss with a partner.

It's a really cool site.

5

A In spoken English, a /w/ sound is sometimes inserted between words in a process known as intrusion. Listen to the example.

> **Example:** I never do any e-mailing. (no intrusion)
> I never do_wany e-mailing. (/w/ intrusion)

B Look at these sentences and predict where you might hear a /w/ intrusion. Now listen and check.

1. I have no online access from this computer.
2. Helen isn't an Internet addict, but you are!
3. Even though I was really tired, I had to go on.
4. Go under the bridge, then go through another tunnel.
5. You and I are going to an event tonight.
6. I have to do another two exercises before I can finish.

C Listen again. Practice with a partner. Can you think of any rules for when /w/ intrusion might take place?

6

A Listen to the lecture and circle the topics the speaker mentions.

> search engines   TV   news   chatting
>
> e-mail   CD-ROM   radio   the Internet

B What advice does the speaker give? Take notes on the memo pad, and then share your notes with a partner.

7

Listen and circle the answers that are right for you.

1. Sure, I use one all the time.	Yeah, I'm OK.	No, I have no idea.
2. Absolutely.	It's not that important.	No way, it's just a fad.
3. All the time.	Occasionally.	Never.
4. Yes, tons.	A couple of times a week.	Never, or almost never.
5. It sure is.	Newspapers are better.	No, it's full of lies.

Your Turn!

Talking about the Internet

- How long do you spend online?
  I usually spend **an hour a day** surfing the Internet and checking e-mail.
- What's your favorite site?
  I really like the **Internet movie database**.
- What's the URL?
  It's **www.imdb.com**
- How often do you visit it?
  I visit it **a few times a week**.
- How many e-mails do you send every day?
  I usually send and receive **about five a day**.

Favorite web sites

_____
_____
_____
_____
_____
_____
_____
_____
_____
_____
_____

Try this . . .

Make a list of your favorite web sites. What is the URL for each? Work with a partner. Discuss why you like these sites. What do you use them for?

In Focus: *What makes a person "human"?*

Can a computer think? In 1950, the British mathematician Alan Turing proposed a test for determining whether a computer was intelligent. In this test, called the Turing Test, a person asks questions to another person and a computer, without knowing which is the person, and which is the computer. In this test, if the person asking the questions is unable to decide which is a real person, then you can call the computer intelligent. When Deep Blue, a computer, beat the world chess champion Garry Kasparov in 1997, many people saw this as evidence that computers had finally become smarter than people. The interesting thing about Deep Blue's victory over Kasparov was not that the computer won the game—being good at chess is a very specialized problem-solving activity, of the sort that suits a computer very well—but Kasparov's reaction. He accused the computer of cheating, and said that there had to be a person controlling its moves. That is, he mistook the computer for a human player. By this definition, then perhaps Deep Blue was intelligent. *Do you think computers will one day be able to think for themselves? Will they have feelings?*

Being good at chess doesn't mean computers are smart. You can't talk to a computer.

I'm sure that one day computers will be more intelligent than people.

Thinking isn't the same as feeling, and computers will never have feelings.

It's a really cool site.

That's a good question.

oals | • Understanding interviews and talk shows
• Identifying advantages and disadvantages

A Use the job titles in the box to label the pictures. One title is extra.

| meteorologist | talk show host | children's show host |
| newscaster | game show host | sportscaster |

_____

_____

_____

_____

_____

B What exactly does each person do? Discuss each person's job responsibilities with a partner.

C Brainstorm! Work with a partner. Which of the program types above do you watch? Who are the best presenters? Make a list. What do you like about them?

2

A Listen to extracts from five shows, and number (1–5) the pictures in Task 1.

B Listen again and make a note of the main points of each extract.

1. _____   4. _____

2. _____   5. _____

3. _____

3

A David Dale, host of *Young World*, is interviewing the host of *Asia Today*, Kathy Koh. Listen and number the questions in the order in which he asks them.

Question:

_____ What makes a person a good host?   •

_____ What do you do?   •

_____ What advice would you give young people?   •

_____ What kinds of topics do your viewers prefer?   •

Answer:

- The host of a current affairs program.
- Need curiosity.
- Asking good questions.
- Conflict.
- Looking straight at the camera.
- Call people up the day before the interview for research.
- Good communication skills.
- Different points of view.
- Thinking quickly.
- A nice-sounding voice.

B Listen again and match the questions with the answers Kathy gives. There may be more than one answer for each question.

4

A The word *that* can be pronounced in two ways—the strong (or dictionary) form, and the weak form. Listen to the two examples from the interview:

> **Example 1:** According to our studies, viewers love that. (strong form)
> **Example 2:** There are two things that you must have. (weak form)

B Look at these sentences. Write *S* where you think *that* will be strong and *W* where you think it will be weak. Listen and check.

1. I don't want this one, I want that (   ) one.

2. I thought that (   ) you weren't coming.

3. I'm not eating that (   ) !

4. It was the best meal that (   ) I've ever eaten.

5. He crashed the car that (   ) he bought last week.

6. That (   ) guy is the man that (   ) gave me the map.

C Listen again and practice. Are there any rules to determine whether *that* is pronounced in the strong or the weak form?

That's a good question.

A David is interviewing four other people from the studio about their jobs. Write each person's job.

Person	Job	Good or Bad	Details
		Good Bad	
		Good Bad	
		Good Bad	
		Good Bad	

B Listen again. Is each person talking about the good or bad points of their job? Circle *Good* or *Bad* and make notes of the things they like or don't like.

Listen and circle the answers that are right for you.

1. Yeah, quite a lot.   An hour or so a day.   No, hardly any.
2. More than twenty.   Ten to twenty.   Less than ten.
3. News or sports.   Movies or dramas.   I don't really watch TV.
4. I'd love to.   It'd be OK, I suppose.   No, it doesn't interest me.
5. Newscaster.   Game show host.   Talk show host.

Your Turn! 🔊

Discussing a talk show

- Who would you invite?
  I'd definitely invite **Julia Roberts**.
  I'd love to interview **Albert Einstein**.
  Bill Gates would be a good person to talk to.
  It would be interesting to talk to **Akira Kurosawa**.
- Why would you choose that person?
  She's **really talented**, and **it would be great to meet her**.
  I'm sure **he'd have a lot of interesting things to say**.
- What would you want to ask?
  I'm interested in **his movies**, and I'd like to **hear him talk about them**.
  What I'd like to know is **where he got all his ideas from**.

Talk Show ———

Guest 1: _____
Why? _____

Questions: _____

Guest 2: _____
Why? _____

Questions: _____

Guest 3: _____
Why? _____

Questions: _____

Try this . . .

Work with a partner. You and your partner are talk show hosts. You can invite onto your show any three people, living or dead. Who would you invite? Why? What questions would you ask them? Tell another pair.

In Focus: *The host with the most*

Perhaps the most successful interviewer of all time would have to be Oprah Winfrey, the host of *The Oprah Winfrey Show*. Her show, which has been running on American daytime television since 1984, is watched by 26 million viewers a week in the United States and is seen in 34 countries. Consistently ranked as the highest paid female entertainer in the United States, Oprah earns around $300 million a year, and in 1998, she broke records by signing the largest ever TV contract. She received $150 million for hosting her show for the 2001/2002 season, and in 2002 she renewed the contract for another two years. Her show has won over 34 Emmy Awards, including seven Emmy Awards to Oprah herself for Outstanding Talk Show Host. In addition, she started Oprah's Book Club, in which she chose a book which she thought would be of interest to her viewers and talked about it. Because of this club 46 titles became best-sellers, and she received a medal from the National Book Foundation for her contribution to reading. *Who are the most successful TV presenters in your country? What makes them popular? How much do you think they earn, and do you think they deserve their salary?*

The best talk show hosts can make their guests feel at ease, so they want to talk freely.

I think TV presenters deserve their high salary, because they work under a lot of pressure.

Talk show hosts are so overpaid. Anyone could do that job!

That's a good question.

Do you have a pet peeve?

Goals
• Understanding interviews
• Identifying solutions

1

A Look at the pictures below. Three of the pictures relate to peeves (dislikes), and three relate to phobias (fears). Circle the appropriate word for each.

peeve / phobia

peeve / phobia

peeve / phobia

peeve / phobia

peeve / phobia

peeve / phobia

B What peeve or phobia do each of these people have? Discuss with a partner.

C **Brainstorm!** Work with a partner. What other peeves or phobias do people have? Make a list for each. Do you have any?

2

 A A psychologist is talking about phobias and peeves. Listen and number the pictures in Task 1A in the order in which you hear them mentioned.

B Listen again and check your answers. According to the speaker, what is a phobia, and what is a peeve? Write definitions.

Phobia _____

_____

Peeve _____

_____

3

 A Listen to four people talking about their phobias. What is each person afraid of?

Listen for it

Freaks me out is an informal way to say something scares you.

Person	Phobia	What do they do?
John		
Tina		
Rebecca		
Sam		

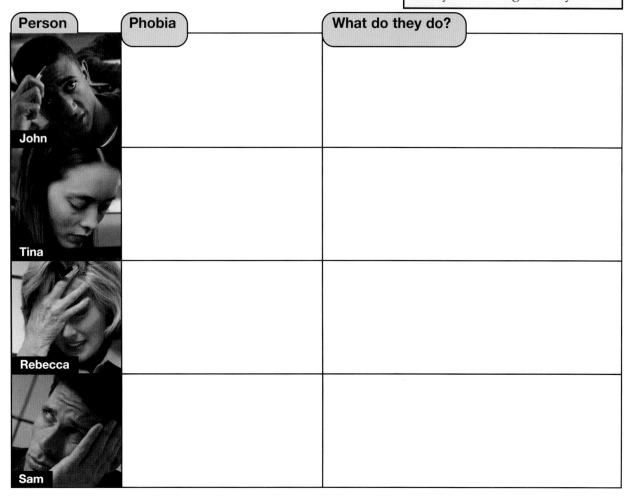

B Listen again. What does each person do about their phobia?

4

A **In spoken English, a /r/ sound is sometimes inserted between words in a process known as intrusion. Listen to the example.**

> **Listen for it**
>
> *Drives me crazy* is an informal way to say you think something (or someone) is really annoying.

> **Example:** I saw eleven movies last month. (no intrusion)
> I saw_releven movies last month. (/r/ intrusion)

B **Look at these sentences and predict where you might hear a /r/ intrusion. Now listen and check.**

1. I don't really care about things like smoking.
2. Law and order is an important issue in this election.
3. Even though animals are interesting, I think plants are more interesting.
4. The area in which he lives is very far away.
5. I saw another four or five movies last week.
6. In English, sheep say "baa" and cows say "moo."

C **Listen again and practice. When do you think /r/ intrusion occurs?**

5

A **Four people are talking about their "pet peeves." Listen and write what annoys each person.**

What peeves them?	What should be done?
1. _____	_____
2. _____	_____
3. _____	_____
4. _____	_____

B **Listen again. Note down what each person thinks should be done. Check your answers with a partner.**

6

Listen and circle the answers that are right for you.

1. No, it doesn't bother me.   Kind of.   I sure do.
2. Oh, it drives me crazy.   It's a bit annoying.   It's never happened to me.
3. Not really.   A few.   Hundreds.
4. It doesn't worry me at all.   Sometimes it bothers me.   Yeah, so do I.
5. Sure I would.   No, I don't believe in them. No, I'd be too embarrassed.

Your Turn! 🔊

Talking about peeves and manners

- It really annoys me when people smoke in restaurants.
  I agree. **I'd make it illegal to smoke in public places.**
  I disagree. I think **people should be allowed to smoke where they want.**
  It doesn't really bother me.
- I'd like to see **talking in the theater made illegal.**
- I hate it when **people drop litter on the street.**
  Yes, I think **litter bugs should be fined, or sent to jail.**
  It's not something I really care about.
- I'd love it if **cell phones were banned on the train.**
- I'd bring in a law to **make honking your car horn illegal.**

Try this . . .

Are there any things in your society that annoy you? Work with a partner. Imagine you and your partner are politicians in your country. What new laws would you introduce, and why? Make a list. Share your list with other pairs. Do they agree with you?

Law	Reason

In Focus: *Fear and loathing*

The American National Institute of Mental Health has estimated that around 10 percent of Americans suffer from phobias. Phobia sufferers experience a range of symptoms, including increased heart beat, sweating, dizziness, and difficulty breathing. Psychiatrists divide phobias into three types: **agoraphobia**, a fear of open, or crowded, spaces; **social phobias**, such as speaking in public; and **specific phobias**, of which the most common are *zoophobia* (a fear of animals—particularly dogs, snakes, insects, and mice), *claustrophobia* (closed spaces), and *acrophobia* (heights). It is the third type that contains the strangest phobias, including *caligynephobia* (a fear of beautiful women), *triskaidekaphobia* (a fear of the number thirteen), and *peladaphobia* (a fear of bald people). *Do you (or anyone you know) have any phobias? What do you think causes phobias? How should we treat people with phobias?*

People with phobias just need some counseling. I think you can get over fears if you try hard enough.

I'm terrified of speaking in public. I could never give a speech to a large group.

I have an uncle who has *coulrophobia*— he's terrified of clowns!

view

Units 11–15

1

A Listen to the eight extracts. Write the number of each extract next to the correct type of listening.

Type of listening		Key words
street directions	_____	_____
directions in a hotel	_____	_____
technical instructions	_____	_____
administrative instructions	_____	_____
news report	_____	_____
weather report	_____	_____
TV talk show	_____	_____
job interview	_____	_____

B Listen again and write the key words that helped you decide.

2

A Listen to the speaker talking about use of e-mail. Circle the things the speaker talks about. Two are extra.

(use of capitals)   (computer viruses)   (subject lines)   (spelling)

(chat rooms)   (grammar)   (attachments)

B Listen again and note the five rules the speaker mentions.

The Five Rules of Netiquette
1. _____
2. _____
3. _____
4. _____
5. _____

3

A A TV interviewer is introducing the guests on tonight's show. Listen and write the topics he will talk about with each one.

Enrique Iglesias	Natalie Portman	Ahn Jung-Hwan
_____	_____	_____
_____	_____	_____
_____	_____	_____

B Listen again and check your answers.
Which of the guests has he interviewed before? _____

4

A Listen to the interview with a TV journalist. What does the journalist talk about? Listen and number the pictures (1–4). One is extra.

B Listen again and circle the aspects of the job the journalist enjoys.

5

Listen and circle the answers that are right for you.

1. The shuttle bus.	The best way is by train.	I'd take a taxi.
2. No, there aren't any.	There's one near here.	Yeah, there are a few.
3. I watch local news the most.	Mostly national news.	I guess international.
4. Yeah, it's really annoying.	It's kind of irritating.	It doesn't really bother me.

Goals | • Identifying attitude
| • Following instructions

1

A Use the words in the box to complete the travel ads. Circle the words in the ads that help you decide.

| diving | climbing | survival | caving |

Travel & Leisure
Tours, Discount Tickets, Re

Adventure Tours ☐

Plunge into the savage domain of the ravenous blue shark!
San Piedras Shark Expeditions gives extreme adventurers the chance to go _____ with these legendary predators.
Call 555-JAWS for details. ☐

Be a subterranean explorer!
Join *Hidden Kingdom Adventures* and descend into the cavernous gorges of the spectacular 6 km-long "Great Cavern." Enjoy an exciting combination of underground abseiling, climbing, and

_____.
Ph: 555-8100

Conquer the icy peaks of the Western Alps. ☐
Join one of our weekly expeditions to some of the most treacherous icefalls in Italy and France. Over 20,000 m of slopes for _____.
Contact *Iceman Tours*: 555-2325

Have you got what it takes? ☐
Live for 30 days in the wilds of the Brazilian rain forest with only your guides to assist you. Sign up now for a Castaway Tours jungle _____ course. **Tel: 1-800-555-7786**

B Use the words below to talk about the adventure vacations described in the ads. Which of the adventures would you choose?

| thrilling | dangerous | terrifying | risky | exhausting | wild | challenging | tough |

C **Brainstorm!** Work with a partner. Do you know any other types of extreme sports or adventure vacations? Make a list. Which of them would you like to try?

2

A Four people are talking about the adventure vacations in Task 1. Listen and number the advertisements in the correct order (1–4).

Listen for it

To play it safe means to avoid taking risks.

B Listen again. Is each person interested in the vacation? If no, write the reason and what the speaker would prefer to do.

	Interested in vacation?		Reason	Prefers
Carmen	Yes	No	_____	_____
Steve	Yes	No	_____	_____
Jin-sook	Yes	No	_____	_____
Glen	Yes	No	_____	_____

3

A An instructor is talking about jungle survival skills. Listen and check (✔) the picture for each topic he discusses.

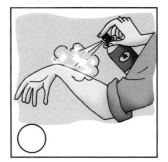

B Listen again. What does the instructor say you should and should not do? Write (✔) or (✗) next to each piece of advice.

_____ Keep containers of food in your tent.

_____ Use the water in rivers for drinking and cooking.

_____ Wear light cotton clothing to stay cool.

_____ Check for animals in the trees as you walk past.

_____ Set up your tent close to a body of water.

_____ Use a stick to probe the ground for snakes.

4

A You can use intonation to mean the opposite of what you say. Listen to the examples.

> **Example:** Oh no, I wasn't scared at all.   (Speaker wasn't scared)
> Oh no, I wasn't scared at all.   (Speaker was scared)

B Now, listen to the sentences and circle the correct meaning. Then listen again and practice.

1. The caving trip . . .	was really exciting.	wasn't exciting.
2. The climbing . . .	was extremely challenging.	wasn't very challenging.
3. The survival course . . .	was very easy.	wasn't very easy.
4. The sky diving . . .	was terrifying.	wasn't terrifying.
5. The diving expedition . . .	was fun.	wasn't fun.

5

Listen for it

In one piece means safe and unhurt after a difficult experience or dangerous journey.

A Listen as Carmen, Glen, and Jin-sook describe some of the things they did on their adventure vacations. Write *C* for Carmen, *G* for Glen, or *J* for Jin-sook in the boxes next to each picture.

  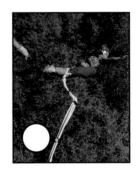 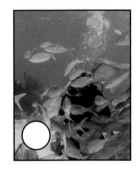

Enjoyed it	Enjoyed it	Enjoyed it	Enjoyed it
Didn't enjoy it	Didn't enjoy it	Didn't enjoy it	Didn't enjoy it

B Listen again. Did the person enjoy that part of their vacation? Circle *Enjoyed it* or *Didn't enjoy it*.

6

Listen and circle the answers that are right for you.

1. Sounds great.	I might be.	Not particularly.
2. Absolutely.	I'm not sure.	No way.
3. Yeah, I'd really like to.	I've considered it.	No, never.
4. That sounds perfect.	That sounds all right.	That sounds really boring.

Your Turn! 🔊

Asking and talking about vacations

- What do you think of **a rafting trip?**
  Yeah, that sounds **exciting**.
- Where should we do it?
  How about **Nepal? The rivers there are pretty challenging**.
- OK, for a **five day** trip, how much should we charge?
  I think **$500** sounds right.
- What about special training or equipment?
  Well, everyone will need **to be able to swim**, and we'll supply **rafts and life jackets**.
- And the exciting features?
  Well, the people on the trip will get to **ride the thrilling wild rivers of Nepal** and they'll see **the spectacular Himalayan scenery**.
- Anything else?
  Yeah, **they'll spend five exhausting and challenging days on the water**.

Where? _____

How long? _____

Cost? _____

Training/equipment needed? _____

_____

Exciting features? _____

_____

Trip name? _____

Try this . . .

Work with a partner. You have just opened a new adventure vacation agency, and you need to come up with an adventure vacation package. Think about the questions on the form, and create a radio ad for your vacation. Listen to other classmates' ads and decide which trip you would like to take.

In Focus: *Games without frontiers*

Along with the prestige that comes with staging the Olympic Games, host cities have in past years been granted the privilege of adding their choice of sports to the line up of events. In 1988, tennis was added at the request of host city Seoul, in 1992 Barcelona was allowed to include baseball and badminton, in 1996 softball was played in Atlanta and in 2000, taekwando and triathlon events were held in Sydney. In the run-up to the 2004 Olympics, however, the International Olympic Committee (IOC) broke this tradition by turning down host city Athens' request to include water-skiing as an event. Though it was unprecedented for the IOC to reject a host city's wishes, it was hardly the first time an event had been denied a place on the Olympic roster. Among many others, racquetball, bowling, billiards, polo, surfing, and even bridge and chess have been candidates—all of them rejected—for inclusion in the Olympics. *How do you feel about the current line-up of Olympic sports? Are there any events that don't deserve a place? Are there any that should be added? What should be the standard for deciding what qualifies as an Olympic sport?*

I don't think events like gymnastics should be included because the results are subjective.

There are still not enough extreme sports in the Olympics, even though they're very popular.

The standard should simply be whether or not there is a clear winner, which means events like figure skating should be dropped.

It has good points and bad points.

G oals | • Identifying arguments for and against an issue
• Listening critically to alternative viewpoints

1

A **Look at the newspaper article. What is planned for Winchester Island?**

The Winchester Herald
Winchester Island's Own Daily Newspaper

Big Resort Planned for WI
by Kate Fletcher

A $260 million development has been planned for Winchester Island. Island Holidays, Inc., one of the five largest resort companies in America, today announced their plan to turn the forest reserve on the east coast of the island into a multi-million dollar five-star resort. "A development like this will breathe new life into Winchester Island," said Ian Rodgers, vice-president of Island Holidays. "This resort will bring people and jobs to the island, while turning it into a world-class tourist attraction."

Some local residents were less excited. Sue Callahan, founder of Save Winchester Island!, said, "This development will destroy one of the last untouched beaches on Winchester Island, and the tourists it brings will crowd our roads and cause all kinds of problems." A meeting is planned for Thursday night between

Ian Rodgers,
vice-president of Island Holidays

B **What are some of the arguments for the resort development? What are some of the arguments against? Work with a partner and make two lists. Can you think of any other arguments for or against the development?**

C **Brainstorm! Work with a partner. Are there any developments near where you live, either proposed or already constructed, that you agree or disagree with? Why do you feel that way?**

2

A Listen to Alan and Cindy discussing the development. Who makes each statement?

Statement	Alan	Cindy
The island is boring.	☐	☐
The island is quiet and peaceful.	☐	☐
More people means more noise.	☐	☐
There'll be windsurfing, volleyball, and golf.	☐	☐
People will have fun.	☐	☐
Trees will be cut down.	☐	☐
Birds and animals will lose homes.	☐	☐
More tourists will come.	☐	☐
The town will get more money.	☐	☐
There'll be more traffic and pollution.	☐	☐
There'll be more jobs.	☐	☐

B Listen again and check your answers. Do you think Cindy and Alan are for the development or against it?

3

A Listen to callers speaking on a radio talk show. Number the callers in the order you hear them speak (1–4).

Listen for it

Go ahead is used to encourage someone to start or continue speaking.

in favor / opposed

in favor / opposed

- more business will bring more money •

- traffic will become worse •

- we won't be able to fish near the resort area •

- more tourists will appreciate the island •

• worried about destruction of resources •

- more money might mean better facilities •

- life will become more difficult •

in favor / opposed

in favor / opposed

B Listen again and match each speaker with their comments. Is each speaker in favor or opposed to the development? Circle the correct answer.

It has good points and bad points. **83**

4

A Representatives of Winchester Island Town Council and Island Holidays are discussing the resort development. Listen and check the problems you hear discussed.

Listen for it

Not to mention is used to add extra information to a point you are making.

Problem
☐ Businesses and jobs will be lost •
☐ People won't be able to go fishing •
☐ Natural resources will be destroyed •
☐ The traffic situation will become worse •
☐ Shops will become too crowded •
☐ More people will try to build hotels and restaurants •

Solution
• The resort will build new roads
• The resort will buy out their businesses
• The town will build a new nature park next to the resort
• They'll be offered jobs at the resort
• The town can afford to build bigger roads
• The resort will build a nature park

B Listen again. Match the problems you checked with a suggested solution.

5

A Listen to how some of the underlined words in the example are changed in rapid speech.

> **Example:** <u>What do you</u> think of the development? (Whaddaya)

B Listen to the sentences and write in the missing words.

1. _____ move to Winchester Island?
2. _____ find out about this resort?
3. _____ do on the weekend?
4. _____ do for fun?
5. _____ next vacation?
6. _____ decide to quit your job?

C Listen again and check your answers. Practice with a partner.

6

Listen and circle the answers that are right for you.

1. A lot.   A little.   Not much at all.
2. It's a good thing.   It's a bad thing.   It depends.
3. Sure, definitely.   I might.   I don't think so.
4. Global warming.   Pollution.   Animal and plant extinction.
5. It's getting better.   It's getting worse.   It's not really changing.

Your Turn! 🔊

Arguing for and against a point

- The problem is that **this resort will bring too many tourists to the island.**

  Yes, but on the other hand, **think of all the money they'll bring.**

  I agree with you, **but there'll be a lot of new jobs.**
- What we're concerned about is **the wildlife in the area that will be killed.**

  That's a good point, but **the resort company will be creating a new forest reserve.**

  I see your point, but **aren't jobs more important than a few birds and insects?**
- Excuse me. Can I just say something here? What about other problems? For example, **what about the fishermen?**
- And another thing, **think of all the new roads the resort company will build.**

☐ For   ☐ Against

REASONS

1. _____
   _____
2. _____
   _____
3. _____
   _____
4. _____
   _____
5. _____
   _____

Try this . . .

Have a debate! Divide into groups. Half the group will work together as supporters of the development on Winchester Island. The other half will be opponents of the development. Write a list of arguments for your side, and examples to support your argument. Then come together with the other team and debate.

In Focus: *Bad news for biodiversity*

A recent survey found that the two environmental issues of greatest concern to the average American are the rate at which land is being developed and places in nature are being lost, and the loss of rain forests. Almost 70 percent of the people surveyed strongly agreed with the statement: "We have a personal responsibility to the earth to protect all plant and animal life." In another survey, by The American Museum of Natural History, 70 percent of scientists interviewed said they believe that during the next thirty years as many as one-fifth of all species alive today will become extinct. A third of the respondents think as many as half the species on Earth will die out in that time. Most of the scientists agree that human activity is the main cause of the problem. Factors such as expanding human settlements, logging, mining, agriculture, and pollution contribute towards destruction of ecosystems, and species extinction. *Are you concerned about environmental issues? Are there other issues that are more important? What (if anything) can the average person do about world problems?*

Jobs are more important than some beetles in a rain forest.

The environment is important, but I think other issues like crime and terrorism are more important.

I don't like to think about things like this. I mean, what can one person do?

I was so embarrassed.

Goals
- Following a narrative
- Identifying feelings and emotions

1

A Look at the words in the box. Do you know what they mean? Ask your partner, or look them up in a dictionary.

apologetic	nervous	frustrated	embarrassed	surprised	confused
amused	annoyed	upset	disappointed	excited	furious

B How does each person feel? Write words from the box above to describe each person's emotion(s).

1. _____
2. _____

3. _____

4. _____
5. _____

6. _____
7. _____

8. _____
9. _____

10. _____

C **Brainstorm!** Work with a partner. What other words or expressions do you know to describe emotions? Are these emotions negative, positive, or neutral? Make three lists.

2

A Listen to three people talking about their first day at work. Number the pictures (1–3).

Main points:

_____

_____

_____

Main points:

_____

_____

_____

Main points:

_____

_____

_____

B Listen again and note the main points of the stories.
Work with a partner. Choose one story and try retelling it to your partner.

3

A Label each picture with one of the words below. One word is extra. Then listen. How does each person feel? Number the pictures in order (1–4).

> **Listen for it**
>
> To *laugh your head off* means to laugh very hard.

apologetic   angry   amused   frustrated   surprised

_____   _____   _____   _____

B Listen again to check your answers.
Work with a partner. Choose one or two of the situations and act them out with your partner.

4

A Listen to five more people talking about their first day at work. How did each speaker feel? Circle the correct feeling.

Listen for it

Anyway has many uses in storytelling, including to return to an earlier point in the story.

1. angry   embarrassed   annoyed

2. excited   apologetic   nervous   4. amused   apologetic   furious

3. annoyed   embarrassed   surprised   5. apologetic   annoyed   frustrated

B Listen again and check your answers. If you had been the person in each situation, what would you have said or done next? Tell your partner.

 5

A Listen to four situations. Are the people apologizing or sympathizing? Circle the correct answer for each.

	Words used
1. apologizing / sympathizing	_____
2. apologizing / sympathizing	_____
3. apologizing / sympathizing	_____
4. apologizing / sympathizing	_____

B Listen again. What words did each person use to express their feelings?

6

A Listen to the following sentences. Write *S* when you hear the strong form of the pronoun, and *W* when you hear the weak form.

> **Example 1:**   I don't like <u>her</u>, but I like him. (strong)
> **Example 2:**   I don't like <u>her</u> at all. (weak)

1. The ball went right over her ( ) head.

2. I waited for the actor to make his ( ) appearance.

3. It's not mine, it's his ( ).

4. You weren't there, so I gave it to him ( ).

5. I can't believe they gave the part to her ( ).

6. I told her ( ) to show him ( ) the gift.

B Listen again and check your answers. Practice with a partner.

 7

Listen. How would you feel in each situation? Circle the answer that's right for you.

1. frustrated   annoyed   upset   4. nervous   upset   embarrassed

2. surprised   confused   frustrated   5. surprised   excited   upset

3. annoyed   frustrated   nervous   6. disappointed surprised   furious

Your Turn! 🔊

Telling a story

- This one time, **I had an important job interview**.
- Well, **I didn't want to be late, so I arrived about 30 minutes early.**
- So, then **I decided to go for a coffee and a snack while I was waiting.**
- After that, **I went to the interview, and I thought it went pretty well.**
- Anyway, **after the interview, I was feeling pretty happy—until I saw myself in a mirror.**
- You know what? **I had spilled coffee and bits of food all over my shirt!**
- So, in the end, **you can imagine how I felt.**

Where? _____

When? _____

Who with? _____

What happened? _____

_____

_____

_____

_____

_____

How did you feel? _____

_____

Try this . . .

Work with a partner, or in a small group. Choose an emotion and write a short conversation or story that demonstrates that feeling. Look at the questions on the form for ideas. Tell another group. They will guess what emotion you've chosen.

In Focus: *What's your EQ?*

Intelligence tests have been used for many years to judge peoples' Intelligence Quotient, or IQ. A much more recent invention, but one which is gaining in popularity, is the measuring of Emotional Intelligence, known as EQ. Emotional Intelligence is divided into five areas: *self awareness*—recognizing your own feelings; *managing emotions*—handling your feelings in an appropriate way, and dealing with negative emotions well; *motivating oneself*—this includes things like self control, and using your emotions to achieve goals; *empathy*—understanding other peoples' feelings, and seeing their point of view; and *handling relationships*—your social skills, and how well you emotionally interact with other people. Many people believe that your Emotional Intelligence is more important than any other intelligence, and is a better predictor of how successful you will be in work, and in life. Some employers have even started giving EQ tests to job applicants. *Do you believe there is such a thing as Emotional Intelligence? How important are tests like IQ and EQ tests? Which of the five areas would you be strongest—and weakest—in?*

I think Emotional Intelligence is just as important as regular intelligence. Maybe more important.

There's no way you can measure someone's emotions like that.

I think I'd get a good score for empathy—I'm good at understanding people's feelings.

What's on TV tonight?

Goals
- Identifying the topic of a monolog
- Following instructions

1

A Read the *TV Highlights* and use the words in the box to label each type of program. Circle the words in the ads that helped you decide.

> game show   sitcom   current affairs show   talk show
> soap opera   cartoon   cooking show   sports show

TV Highlights

Mr. Nutty ( )
The wacky Mr. Nutty is up to his crazy tricks again. Tune in for laughs every Sunday at 8 on SBC.

Open Mike ( )
Join host Mike Barber for interviews with some of the biggest names in movies and sports. KBC at 8 p.m.

Center Ice ( )

All the latest ice hockey headlines and highlights are right here every night. Hosted by Dirk Grady. 9 p.m. on Channel Q.

The Smiling Chef ( )
Everyone's favorite chef, Sawyer Kane, visits an organic farm, and shows how to make French Onion Quiche and Blueberry Scones. TV-25 at 8 p.m.

Krazy Kritters ( )
Wild, wacky, and witless, the far-out creatures of Zippety Zoo are ready to entertain kids of all ages. Kids-TV at 8.

Face the Issues ( )
Every week, our panel of experts addresses the political and economic problems making headlines. 11 p.m. on TV-25.

Trauma Ward ( )

Follow the lives and loves of the doctors and nurses in the critical care ward at Eagleton General. BTV at 8.

Roll 'Em ( )
Watch all the fun as three contestants vie for $50,000 in prize money every week. On Channel Q at 8:00 p.m.

B Which of the programs above would you be most interested in watching? Share your choices and reasons with a partner.

C **Brainstorm!** Work with a partner. Think of at least five more types of TV shows and give an example of each.

A Imagine it is 8:15 p.m. Listen to someone flipping through TV channels, and number the channels in the order you hear them.

BTV	SBC	TV-25	KBC	Kids-TV	Channel Q
Prime Time Highlights					
7:00 Fashion Central	**7:00** SBC NewsWatch	**7:00** Money World	**7:00** Face the Issues	**7:00** My Strange Family	**7:00** Legal Defense
7:30 Cop Town	**7:30** Celebrity Profile		**7:30** The Week in Politics		**7:30** Inside Story
8:00 Trauma Ward	**8:00** Mr. Nutty	**8:00** The Smiling Chef	**8:00** Open Mike	**8:00** Krazy Kritters	**8:00** Roll 'Em
	8:30 Time & Tide		**8:30** School's Out	**8:30** The Ant Men	
9:00 Tennis Highlights		**9:00** Nature: Lions of the Serengeti		**9:00** Spaced Out	**9:00** Center Ice
		10:00 Movie: To the Quick			

B Listen again and write the key words that helped you decide.

1. _____   4. _____

2. _____   5. _____

3. _____

A TV chef Sawyer Kane is giving instructions on how to make French onion quiche. Listen and check (✔) the ingredients you need.

Listen for it

To die for is an informal way of saying something or someone is extremely desirable.

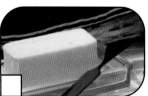

B Listen again and put the cooking instructions in the order you hear them (1–6).

____ sauté the onions   ____ boil the mixture   ____ prepare the pie crust

____ stir the mixture   ____ add spices   ____ pour mixture into pie crust

What's on TV tonight? 91

4

A Intonation can be used to express interest. Listen to the examples.

> **Example:** Oh, is that on tonight? (Sounds interested)
> Oh, is that on tonight? (Sounds uninterested)

B Now, listen and write *I* for *Interested* or *U* for *Uninterested* for each sentence. Then listen again and practice.

____ 1. You're going to watch that movie tonight, aren't you?

____ 2. What time does it start?

____ 3. Oh, is this on again?

____ 4. Oh, it's the one where they go to Las Vegas.

____ 5. You don't want to watch it?

____ 6. It's that new show they've been advertising.

5

A Jerry and Elaine are talking about the TV shows they want to watch. Listen and circle the shows that they talk about.

> ### Listen for it
>
> *Oh, please* is used informally and usually sarcastically to express disbelief or amusement at something someone has said.

TV Guide

BTV World	ABC Pearl	KTV
4:30 Kids' World	**4:00** Kids Rule	**4:25** Money and Stocks
6:30 Easy Cooking	**5:00** The Week in Politics	**4:30** Asia Weekly
6:55 PGA Golf Update	**5:30** Aerobics for You	**5:00** Financial Update
7:00 Wonders Never Cease— An Inside Look at Tokyo	**6:30** News and Weather	**5:30** News and Weather
7:25 Business Report	**7:00** Winner Takes All	**6:00** Stories in the News
7:30 News and Weather	**7:30** Inspector Morse	**6:30** Football Spotlight
8:00 Inside Fashion	**8:30** Space Journey	**8:30** Movie: Bitter Harvest
8:30 NBA Game of the Week	**9:25** News Update	**10:55** News Update
10:00 News	**9:30** The Rolling Stones — Live in Concert	**11:00** Asian Economic Review
10:30 Tennis: Grand Slam Matches	**11:00** Movie: Ghosts in the Attic	

B Listen again. Who wants to see each show? Write *J* for *Jerry* or *E* for *Elaine* next to each show you checked.

6

Listen and circle the answers that are right for you.

1. Yeah, a few hours a day.   I sometimes do.   No, not really.

2. Yeah, there are loads.   There are a few.   There are hardly any.

3. They're really interesting.   They're all right.   They're pretty boring.

4. Sure, it would be fun.   I guess so.   No, I wouldn't.

Your Turn! 🔊

Talking about TV programs

- **What type of show are you planning to make?**
  It's a **situation comedy set at a movie studio.**
- **Could you give me an idea of what it's about?**
  It's about **a young executive trying to stay honest in a corrupt business.**
- **Who do you plan to have on the show?**
  I'd like the main character to be played by **Leonardo di Caprio.**
- **What's the target audience for your show?**
  Mostly people between the ages of **18 and 25.**
- **Why do you think people would want to watch it?**
  It'll be a hit because **everybody's interested in movies and movie stars.**
- **Is there anything else you can tell me about the show?**
  It'll be **funny but it will also deal with serious issues.**

Type of show? _____

What's it about? _____
_____
_____
_____
_____

Who's on it? _____

Who will watch it? _____

Why will people watch it? _____
_____
_____

Try this . . .

Work with a partner. Think of an idea for a TV show that you could propose to a local network. Describe your idea to a partner and answer any questions about the show. Then, switch roles.

In Focus: *Better than the real thing?*

One of the biggest trends in television in recent years has been the rise of "Reality TV." These shows, in which ordinary people are placed in unusual situations and then filmed without a script, have become some of the highest rating shows on television. Early programs of this genre, including *Big Brother* (from the Netherlands) and *Survivor* (from the United States), have led to dozens of copycat programs in many different countries. A common element to many of these programs is that a number of contestants are placed in a closed environment in which they are filmed 24 hours a day, and every week contestants are thrown off the show. What is it about these shows that makes them so popular? Perhaps it is because viewers enjoy watching ordinary people with real emotions being placed in extraordinary situations. Or perhaps it is that people are really voyeurs—they enjoy being a spy, looking secretly into other people's lives. *What do you think of this kind of show? Are reality shows popular in your country? Would you ever consider being a contestant on one of them?*

> When I watch these shows, I really get involved in the contestants' lives. I feel like they're my friends.

> This kind of program should be banned. It just encourages people to be mean to each other.

> I'd love to be a contestant on one. It'd be a great way to get famous quickly.

What's on TV tonight?

I hear what you're saying.

Goals | • Understanding a scientific explanation
• Following an academic lecture

1

A Label the picture with the sense words in the box.

| smell | taste | touch | hearing | sight |

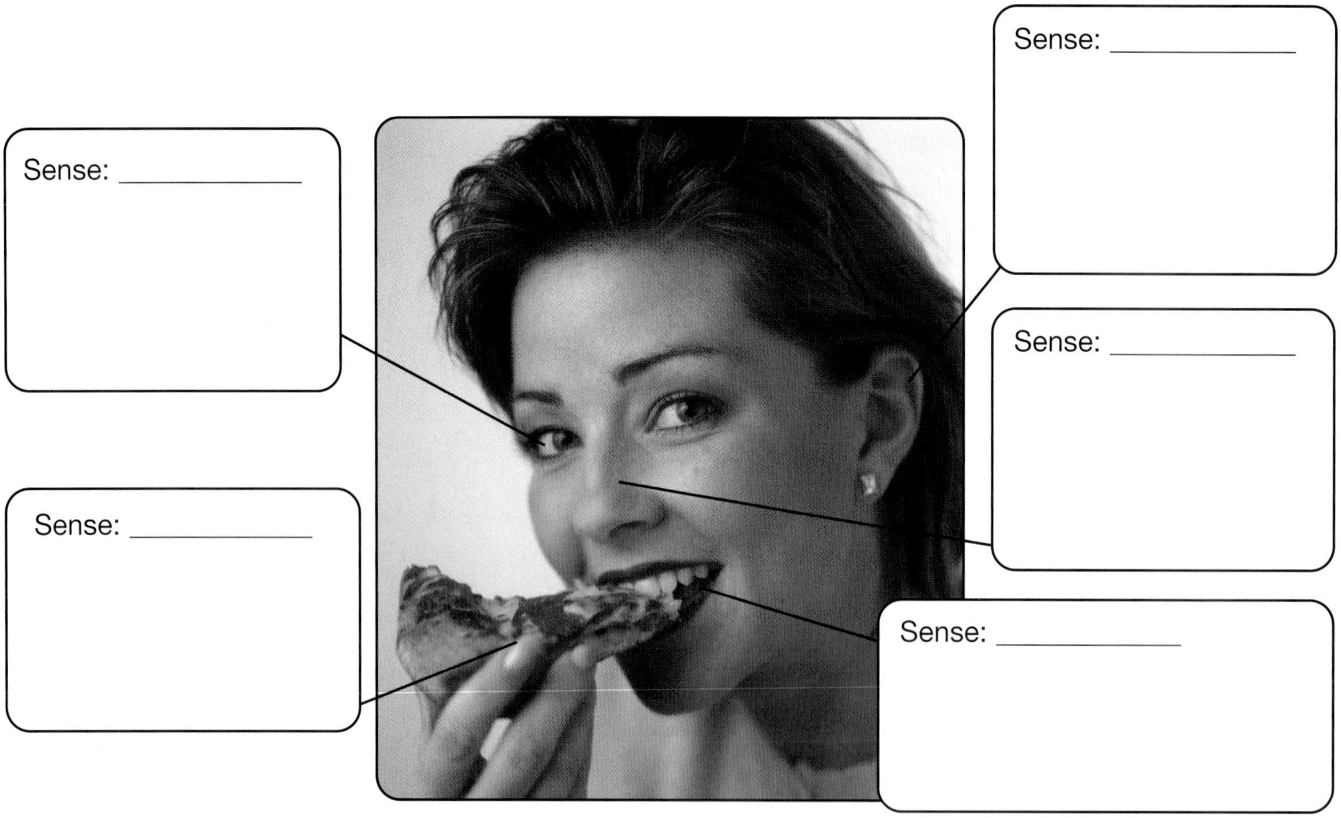

Sense: _____

Sense: _____

Sense: _____

Sense: _____

Sense: _____

B Look at the words below. Which sense is each word associated with? Write each one in the most appropriate box.

| deaf | blind | smooth | paralyzed | colorful | loud | sweet | bitter | aroma |
| scent | rough | perfume | sniff | listen | salty | bright | sour | feel |

C **Brainstorm!** Work with a partner. Are there any other words you can think of that go with the five senses? Add them to the lists above.

A Listen to extracts from five conversations. Which sense is each speaker talking about?

Sense	Key words
1. _____	_____
2. _____	_____
3. _____	_____
4. _____	_____
5. _____	_____

B Listen again. What key words helped you decide?

A A lecturer is talking about how we hear. Listen and use the words in the box to label the parts of the ear.

Listen for it

To tell you the truth is used to show you are saying something honestly, and without hiding anything.

> cochlea   ear canal   hammer   eardrum   anvil
> outer ear   auditory nerve   stirrup   Eustachian tube

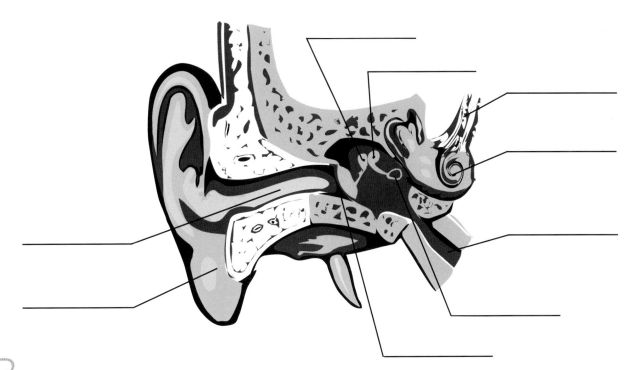

B Listen again and check your answers.

I hear what you're saying.

95

4

A Listen to a lecturer describing how to find your blind spot. Follow the lecturer's instructions. Does it work for you?

Listen for it

Oddly enough and *strangely enough* are used at the start of a sentence to introduce an unusual or interesting fact.

B Listen again and choose the best answers.

1. The light receptors at the back of your eye are on your _____.

   a. eye   **b.** retina   **c.** optic nerve

2. Messages are carried from your eye to your brain by your _____.

   a. retina   **b.** optic nerve   **c.** fovea

3. The blind spot effect is caused because . . .

   a. there is a hole in your eye.   **c.** there are no receptors in one place on your retina.

   b. your fovea is on your retina.

5

A Listen to the way *of* is pronounced in the example sentences.

> **Example 1:** Would you like a cup of tea? (weak)
> **Example 2:** It was just something I thought of. (strong)

B Listen to the way *of* is said in the following sentences, and write *W* for weak form, and *S* for strong form.

1. It was a waste of money. _____

2. Could you pass me that piece of paper? _____

3. There's a new restaurant I heard of. _____

4. How about a glass of wine? _____

5. The leg of the table needs to be fixed. _____

6. That's something I would never have dreamed of. _____

6

Listen and circle the answers that are right for you.

1. Sure, I think so.	Probably.	No, I'm not sure myself.
2. Yeah, I'm pretty sure I do.	Kind of.	No, I've got no idea.
3. Sure, I know a few.	One or two.	No, not really.
4. Taste.	Smell.	I'd miss them both.
5. Listen to music.	Watch a view.	Eat a meal.

Your Turn! 🔊

Giving advice for listening

- I recommend **joining an English conversation class and practicing with the other students.**
- It's a good idea to **watch English TV,** or **listen to English radio every day.**
- The most important thing is **to keep practicing. It gets easier the more you practice.**
- All you need to do is **move to an English-speaking country for a few months.**
- The best advice I could give someone is to **listen to English as often as you can. Being a good listener takes time.**

Listening tips

_____
_____
_____
_____
_____
_____
_____
_____
_____
_____
_____
_____

Try this . . .

Work with a partner. Now that you've almost finished this book, what advice would you give to someone who wanted to improve their English listening ability? Make a list and share it with other pairs. Who has the best advice?

In Focus: _The sixth sense_

In addition to the five normal senses, many people believe in a sixth sense. This sense, often called ESP (Extrasensory Perception), generally falls into one of seven major groups: _telepathy_—the ability to know what someone else is thinking, _clairvoyance_—the ability to "see" things happening in another place, _precognition_—being able to see into the future, _retrocognition_—being able to see far into the past, _mediumship_ or _channeling_—talking to the spirits of dead people, _psychometry_—knowing information about a person or event by touching an object, and _telekinesis_—being able to move things using only your mind. Does the sixth sense exist? Until 1998 Sony had an ESP research department which spent seven years researching the sixth sense. They claim to have proved that ESP does exist, but the study was closed down because there was no way of making money from it. However, one American skeptic, James Randi, has offered $1 million to anyone who can prove ESP exists. No one has yet been able to win the money. _Do you believe in ESP? Have you ever met anyone who claimed to have a sixth sense? Which kind of ESP do you find most interesting?_

> Sure I believe in ESP. Just because we can't see something, doesn't mean it doesn't exist.

> I'm a real skeptic. If ESP is real, how come it's never been proven scientifically?

> I have an aunt who says she can tell the future using tea leaves. There may be some truth in it.

I hear what you're saying.

view

Units 16–20

1

A Listen. Which of these topics are the people talking about? Write the correct letter (a–e) for each one. Some topics will be used more than once.

> a. vacation activities   b. the environment   c. feelings   d. television   e. listening skills

Topic	Key Words
1. _____	_____
2. _____	_____
3. _____	_____
4. _____	_____

Topic	Key Words
5. _____	_____
6. _____	_____
7. _____	_____
8. _____	_____

B Listen again and write the key words that helped you decide.

2

A Listen and number the pictures (1–4).

B Listen again and answer the questions.

1. Where did the event occur? _____

2. What did he do today? _____

3. What decision is made? _____

4. How did she feel? _____

3

A Listen to five TV previews. Number the shows in the order you hear them described. One is extra.

Tonight's TV highlights

Weekly Insight TBN-1 7:30
According to latest estimates, more than one in five teenagers in this country is addicted to the Net. Dale Adams investigates the growing problem of Internet addiction among today's generation of computer-savvy teens.

The Chat Room ABN 11:00
Join host Elisa Grant in her new talk show. Tonight's guests include Formula One racing legend Michael Schumacher. Also, live by satellite, an interview with movie stars Tom Hanks and Jet Li, who talk about their first on-screen movie collaboration.

The Senses: Listening Channel X 9:30
The fourth in this five-part documentary series focuses on our remarkable ability to make sense of the noise around us. Using ground-breaking computer simulations, this program shows for the first time just how the human ear actually works.

Global Watch Environment Channel 8:00
In this week's environmental update, reporter Jane Tennison reports on the plight of the wild tiger and its struggle against extinction. Features stunning footage of a mother tiger giving birth to twin cubs in the snowy wastes of Siberia.

Face Your Fears The Wonder Channel 8:30
Six brave contestants volunteer for the ultimate test of courage and endurance. Tonight's series of challenges includes a white-water rafting trip, a 50-meter bungee-jump, and a close encounter with some angry piranha fish!

B The TV listings above contain some mistakes. Listen again and correct the errors. Then discuss with a partner: Which show would you be most interested in watching? Why?

4

Listen to the questions and note answers that are right for you. Then discuss your answers with a partner.

1. _____

2. _____

3. _____

4. _____

5. _____

Language Summaries

Talking about personal qualities
- How would you describe Jim?
  I'd say aggressive, definitely.
- What qualities do you like in a person?
  I like people who are generous.

Scolding people
- Don't be so selfish!
- Don't be impatient.

Talking about likes and dislikes
- The thing I hate the most is jealousy
- The quality I like most is patience.

Agreeing with someone to an extent
- Would you describe yourself as selfish?
  Well, maybe just a little.
- Wouldn't you say you're kind?
  OK, if you say so.
- Do you think your friends consider you generous?
  I guess.

Unit 2

Talking about gifts
- I still haven't decided what to get him.
  Those ties would really suit him.
- What does he need?
  I'm sure he could use a tie.
- What should we get for Julia?
  I got her a pen.
  How about a computer?
- I can't wait to see his face when he opens the package.

Talking about responsibilities
- Who's taking care of the cake?

Talking about relationships
- They haven't spoken to each other in years.
  Yeah, they've really lost touch.

Expressing annoyance
- Oh, for heaven's sake.

Expressing pleasure
- That's wonderful!

Unit 3

Talking about jobs
- What do you do? / What do you do for a living?
  I'm an accountant.
  I drive a truck.
  I work for a TV studio.

Identifying job responsibilities
- What do you do at work?
  I do research and write scripts.
- What does your job involve?
  I manage the light and sound.
- What are your job responsibilities?
  I check the sound levels and make sure the lights are OK.

Introducing people
- Henry, this is Greg Lorenzo. He's from Moorbridge High School.
- Greg, come and meet Janelle Lee.
- Nice to meet you, Greg.
  Nice to meet you, too.

Unit 4

Making polite requests
- Could you exchange these for me?
- Do you think I could exchange it for another one?
- I wonder if I could exchange these, please?
- Could I please get a larger pair?

Talking about clothes and fashion
- What do you think?
  Looks great! It fits perfectly.
  That dress looks great on you.
  That belt goes really well with that skirt.

Complaining about clothes
- They're too tight.
- The hem's come down.
- A button's come off.
- The stitching is coming undone.
- They're the wrong size.

Asking someone to wait
- Just a moment.

Unit 5

Describing everyday objects
- Chopsticks are used for picking up food.
- You use a corkscrew to open bottles of wine.

Using vague descriptions
- Can you pass me that thing?
- I want to buy one of those things for boiling water.

Asking for the name of an object
- What's this thing called?
- Do you know what this is called?

Expressing agreement
- Fine with me.
- OK, sure. Why not?

Showing understanding
- I know what you mean.

Unit 6

Distinguishing between varieties of English
- "Toilet" isn't a good word to use.
- Where I come from it's called the ground floor.

Asking and talking about vocabulary

- How do you say "toilet" in American English?
- What word do you use for "toilet" in American English?
  We say "restroom."
  We call it a restroom.
- What do you call a sidewalk in British English?
- What's "sidewalk" in British English?
- What's the British word for "sidewalk"?
  It's a pavement.
  It's called a pavement.

Expressing strong agreement

- Sure do! / Sure am! / Sure is!
- Oh, absolutely!

Unit 7

Expressing disapproval

- I ordered some things from the shopping channel.
  You did? Oh, no!
- Look—I got a talking scale.
  But we already have one that works perfectly well.
- We won't need to go to the barber any more.
  If you think I'm going to let you cut my hair, forget it!

Advertising a product

- The great thing is it's so easy to use.
- I know you're going to love this.
- I have the perfect solution for you.
- Losing weight has never before been so easy, or so fun.
- If you like music, you're going to love FreeSound.

Disagreeing with someone

- So, you spent $200 on things we don't need.
  Well, I wouldn't say that.

Unit 8

Reporting what someone has said

- In sports news today, it was announced that . . .
- The 21-year-old students said that . . .
- According to reports for the Pacific Rim Research Institute, . . .

Talking about business data

- In May, we only had $3.5 million in sales.
- In June, we did $6 million.
- We only got $12.5 million in May.
- In June, we brought in $11 million.
- April sales showed continued high growth.
- An increase of $12 million brings us to a total of $36 million.
- In June, we enjoyed an increase of $10 million.
- Our total so far this year is $24 million.

Asking someone to do something for you

- I'd like to see a marketing report on my desk by Monday.

Unit 9

Understanding a sequence of events

- At first things were going fine, until I turned the wrong way.
- What happened next?
  Well, then the instructor told me to pull over.
- After all that, the instructor told me to drive back to the school.

Talking on the phone

- Shane Driving School. Carol speaking
  Oh, hi. I wanted to get some information on driving lessons.
  Oh, hello. I just wanted to find out when my next lesson is.
- You've reached 555-1234. I can't come to the phone right now, but if you leave your number, I'll get right back to you.

Hi, this is Shirley Lim. Could you call me back? My number is . . .

- This is Kelly at Shane Driving School. Can I speak to Shirley Lim, please?
  Speaking.

Talking about traffic incidents

- I turned the wrong way down a one way street.
- I scraped the side of the car really badly.
- I ran right up onto the sidewalk and into a streetlight.
- I ran into the front of the truck.
- The police officer gave me a ticket.

Giving instructions

- Make sure you honk before you back up.
- Just remember—don't drive faster than 5 mph.
- Don't forget to release the parking brake.

Unit 10

Making travel arrangements

- Could I make a reservation, please?
  May I have your departure date?
  I'm sorry but there are no seats available on that date.
- Is that a one-way or round-trip ticket?
- Would you prefer first, business, or economy class?
- Would you like a window or an aisle seat?
- Will that be cash or credit card?
- I'd like to reconfirm my reservation.
- Can I check my reservation?

Identifying schedule information

- Flight 890 leaves Singapore at 8:00 a.m., and arrives at Narita, at 3:45 p.m., connecting with 807 departing from Narita at 6:30 p.m. and arriving at San Francisco at 11:40 a.m.

Apologizing for a delay

- I'm sorry to keep you waiting.

Saying that you'll do something

- I need to change my reservation.
  That's no problem. Leave it to me.

Unit 11

Understanding directions

- Could you recommend a good place to eat?
  Sure, Carmichael's Seafood is nearby.
- What's the best way to get there? / How would I get there?
  Go up Dundas St. to Richmond and turn left.
- Do you know a good park around here?
  Sure, City Park is just past the museum, on your left.
- Is there a car rental agency nearby?
  There's one on 8th Avenue. Take the next left, and you'll see it on your right.
- Is there a gallery around here?
  Yeah, there's one about two streets down on your right. You can't miss it.

Talking about time and distances

- How far's the airport from the city?
  It's about a 40-minute trip.

Ending a conversation with a stranger

- Well, it's been great talking to you, Ed.
  Yeah, see you around, Hideki.

Responding to suggestions

- Take a look at the fitness center.
  Sounds good.
- Wander around the hotel for a while.
  Yeah, I guess I could do that.

Showing you understand instructions

- We're in Union Square right here.
  Oh, I see.
- Go north until you get to Washington Street.
  Looks easy enough.
- From Chinatown, take Jackson Street.
  OK, that's not too hard so far.
  Thanks a lot. I shouldn't have any trouble finding my way.

Unit 12

Making plans to meet

- Hey, you want to get together for lunch tomorrow?
  Great idea. How about noon?
- OK, just don't be late. I've got to leave at 1:30.
  No problem. See you then.

Following a sequence of events

- First, I'm going to get my school ID.
- And then, I'm going to pay my tuition fee.
- And after that, I'm going to register for my classes.
- Then I'll go buy my books.
- And by that time it should be time for lunch.

Emphasizing information to someone

- The campus is pretty big, you know.

Showing you don't understand something

- Hand this to the person over there, with your receipt.
  I'm sorry . . . receipt?
- Can I have your class registration form?
  Excuse me?

Talking about completing a task

- Did you get that done?

Unit 13

Talking about time and frequency

- How often do you visit your favorite site?
  A few times a week.
- How much time do you spend on the Internet?
  About three hours a day on average.
  I surf the Web. That takes about 30 minutes.
- And the rest of the time?
  Then I spend another 30 minutes writing e-mails.

Using "The _____ thing is . . ." to emphasize a point

- The best thing about the e-mail is being able to shop from home.
- The main thing I do on the Internet is study.
- The annoying thing with the Internet is all the spam.

Ending a list

- That's about it really.

Giving an approximation

- How long do you spend e-mailing?
  Say around 10 minutes a day.
  On average, about 15 minutes.

Unit 14

Giving a list of examples

- Well, I think it takes two things for someone to be a good host.
- First, you have to be able to look straight into the camera. That's one part.
- As for the other part, you have to be a good listener.
- There are two things you must have to become a TV show host.
- The first is curiosity.
- And then I think second is being able to communicate well with other people.

Talking about job likes and dislikes

- So, what do you like the most about your job?
  I guess it's meeting famous people.
- So, what's the most boring thing about your job?
  Probably sitting around waiting for the action to start.
- What's the worst thing about your job?
  Having to go to bed early.
- What do you like the least about your job?
  I guess having to do silly things on screen.

Checking information

- So, you probably have to do a lot of research, right?
  Oh, my, yes.

Giving information the listener already knows

- Well, as you know, I'm the host of the show.

Unit 15

Talking about dislikes

- I hate it when people litter on the street.
- I would love it if cell phones were banned.
- It annoys me when people smoke in restaurants.

Empathizing with someone

- I hate flying. I can't stand it.
  Oh, that must be really hard for you, traveling with your job.
- I was really scared of getting into elevators.
  That must have been a real problem.

Asking for examples

- A phobia is a very deep fear of something.
  Such as?
  Can you give me some examples?

Giving an unexpected response

- As a matter of fact, I do have a phobia.
- Well, actually, I'm terrified of spiders.

Emphasizing an opinion

- There certainly are some strange people in the world.
  Yeah, there sure are.

Identifying solutions

- So what did you do about it?
- How did you get over it?
- How did you overcome the problem?

Unit 16

Indicating preferences

- I'd rather take a couple of weeks and go to a beach.
- I'd prefer not to spend my vacation in the freezing cold.
- Boating or water-skiing would be a whole lot better.

Declining an invitation

- Are you sure you don't want to come?
  Yeah, I'm sure. Sorry, I just don't think it's the kind of thing I'd enjoy.

Responding to a declination

- Well, let me know if you change your mind.
- That's OK. I understand.

Giving instructions and warnings

- The first thing to remember is that the weather here is unpredictable.
- The first task ahead of us is to probe for snakes.
- After you do that, make sure your tent is protected.
- For heaven's sake, don't eat food inside the tent.
- Make sure you never set up your tent close to a body of water.
- Whatever you do, don't take your eyes off the ground.

Giving surprising information

- You won't believe this, but I actually spent a month in the jungle.

Unit 17

Arguing for and against a point

- The problem is that the resort will bring too many tourists.
  Yes, but on the other hand, think of all the money they'll bring.
  I agree with you, but there'll be a lot of new jobs.
- What I'm concerned about is the wildlife that will be killed.
  That's a good point, but the resort will make a new forest reserve.
  I see your point, but aren't jobs more important than animals?
- What about other problems? For example, what about the fishermen?
- And another thing, think of all the new roads.

Interrupting a debate

- Excuse me, can I just say something here?

Emphasizing your point

- It's not going to be nice, I can tell you that.
- Our town is going to experience a lot more traffic, and frankly, it's going to make our lives more difficult.

Adding additional points to your argument

- The resort will destroy a lot of beautiful land, not to mention taking away the homes of many birds and animals.
- The nature park will not only be kept clean and beautiful, but will also include educational tours.

Closing your argument

- That's all I have to say.

Unit 18

Starting a story
- Well, it was my very first day, and I had a class of eight kids . . .
- It was the very first night . . .
- Well, it was my first day on the job . . .
- Well, I'd just graduated from school, and had just gotten my first teaching job . . .
- Well, on my first day, they asked me to type up some notes . . .
- I'd just gotten through my first day at work, and I was tired and . . .

Telling a story
- This one time, I had an important job interview.
- Well, I didn't want to be late, so I arrived about 30 minutes early.
- So, then I decided to go for a coffee and a snack while I was waiting.
- After that, I went to the interview, and I thought it went pretty well.
- Anyway, after the interview, I was feeling pretty happy—until I saw myself in a mirror.
- You know what? I had spilled coffee and bits of food all over my shirt!
- So, in the end, you can imagine how I felt.

Using "anyway" to move a story along
- Anyway, I hit it straight at her . . .
- Anyway, I came around a corner too fast . . .
- Anyway, I got on a wrong bus . . .
- Anyway, I typed the notes in time . . .
- Anyway, for some reason, I'd decided to straighten up my desk . . .

Switching to present tense when telling a story to add excitement
- Anyway, I was standing there and this guy comes in . . .
- So this guy cuts in line in front of me, and I say to him . . .

Unit 19

Giving a series of instructions
- First, sauté the onions.
- The next step is to add your other ingredients.
- Now, stir the mixture.
- Then, finally, slide into the oven.

Expressing interest
- That sounds interesting.
- I've always wanted to see it.
- I was hoping to watch the basketball game.
- I wouldn't mind watching the concert.

Describing a TV program
- What type of show is it?
  It's a situation comedy.
- Where's it set?
  In a movie studio.
- What's it about?
  It's about a young executive trying to stay honest in a corrupt business.
- Who's in it?
  No one famous.

Unit 20

Following an academic lecture
- Today I'm going to talk about . . .
- We'll start off by looking at . . .
- Then we'll move on to . . .
- After that we'll cover . . .
- And then, at the end, I'll go over . . .

Asking for someone's attention
- OK, could I have your attention, please?
- Could you please stop talking?
- Quiet, please.

Directing attention to a visual aid
- OK, if you just look at the diagram on the board . . .
- In this diagram you can see the human eye.
- Alright, could you please look at the picture on the next page?

Asking a lecturer a question
- Could I just ask a question?
- I was just wondering.
- Sorry, I didn't quite understand that bit about . . .
- Could you please go over that last bit again?

Listening Skills Index

Welcome to the Self-Study Practice section of *Listen In.* This section of the book will give you extra practice with the target language and listening strategies used in the main units of *Listen In.* In order to complete the Self-Study Practice section, you need to use the Self-Study Practice CD on the inside back cover of this book.

The Self-Study Practice section is made up of 20 separate units. Each one-page unit has the same titles, goals, and target language as one of the 20 main units of *Listen In.* The units in the Self-Study Practice section should be completed one at a time, and only after you have covered the material in the matching main unit in class.

Each unit in the Self-Study Practice section consists of two tasks. The listening passage for each task is recorded on a separate track of the Self-Study Practice CD. See page 128 for a full listing of the CD tracks.

Here is what to do for every unit in the Self-Study Practice section:

Task 1, Part A: There are six questions or statements on the Self-Study Practice CD for this section. For each one, you will find three possible responses listed on the page. Read the list of responses and then listen to the CD. Decide which is the best response for each question or statement and circle the letter (a, b, or c).

For example, you hear:
1. *Excuse me. Are you Jason Lee?*

You see:
1. **a.** Nice to meet you, Jason.
   b. No, I'm Terry Phillips.
   c. Hi, Mr. Lee.

The best response is *No, I'm Terry Phillips.*, so for this question you should circle "b."

Task 1, Part B: Listen to the questions or statements again, along with the correct response to each one. Check to make sure your answers are correct.

Task 2, Part A: The listening passage is a longer dialog or monolog, such as a conversation, an announcement, or a radio broadcast. First, read the instructions and the questions you need to answer. Each unit features one of five question types: (1) Listen and circle the best answer, (2) Listen and circle *T* for *True*, *F* for *False*, or *U* for *Unknown*, (3) Listen and check, (4) Listen and circle the correct items, and (5) Listen and number. Think about what kind of information you will need to listen for. Then listen and complete your answers.

Task 2, Part B: Carefully read the instructions. Think about what type of information you need to listen for (names, descriptions, locations, etc.) and how you need to fill in your answers (filling in a chart, report, memo, advertisement, etc.). Play the dialog or monolog in Part A again and complete your answers.

Some listening tips:
- Complete the Self-Study Practice section in a quiet place with no distractions.
- Try to predict the words you need to listen for and make a list before you begin.
- Don't try to understand every word, just listen for the information you need.
- If you don't get all the information after listening twice, play the track again.

Good luck!

UNIT

He's the generous type.

Student CD Track: **2**

A Listen and circle the best response.

1. **a.** Yeah, he's quite gentle.
   b. Yeah, he really wants to get ahead.
   c. Really? I've never seen him lie.

2. **a.** I know, she never lets him go out alone.
   b. She sure is—she's beautiful.
   c. Yeah. She never shares anything.

3. **a.** I'm sorry. I shouldn't be so selfish.
   b. I'm sorry. Sometimes I'm too aggressive.
   c. You're right. I'm a bit jealous.

4. **a.** Yeah, she should know the answers.
   b. Yeah, she speaks too quickly.
   c. Yeah, I wish she'd hurry up.

5. **a.** I know, I have trouble controlling my temper.
   b. Thanks, that's good of you to say.
   c. That's a bit rude, don't you think?

6. **a.** Really? I thought she was a bit selfish.
   b. Yeah, she can't keep her mouth closed.
   c. Yes. She mustn't want that promotion.

B Listen again and check your answers.

Student CD Track: **3**

A Listen to Jake talking to his doctor. Who does Jake have problems with? Circle the person's relationship with Jake under each picture.

boss / father

_____

girlfriend / sister

_____

mother / teacher

_____

B Listen again. Use an adjective from the box to describe each person's personality, and write it under their photo.

| impatient | nervous | generous | jealous | selfish | aggressive | kind |

UNIT

We could get him a tie.

Student CD Track: **4**

 Listen and circle the best response.

1. **a.** I love it.
   b. It's new.
   c. It was a gift.

2. **a.** Is it new?
   b. He'll love it.
   c. Are you sure?

3. **a.** But they're not family.
   b. I think they should.
   c. Is it Mr. Smith's party?

4. **a.** No, it's too cheap.
   b. That's a generous present.
   c. I went there last year.

5. **a.** No, it's too cheap.
   b. No, it's too late.
   c. No, it's too old.

6. **a.** It's Swiss.
   b. It was new.
   c. It was a present.

B **Listen again and check your answers.**

Student CD Track: **5**

A **Listen and circle the best answer.**

1. **The two people talking are . . .**
   a. brother and sister.
   b. classmates.
   c. teacher and student.

2. **They are deciding on . . .**
   a. a birthday gift.
   b. a wedding gift.
   c. an anniversary gift.

3. **At the end, they decide to get . . .**
   a. a wallet.
   b. a watch.
   c. a pen.

B **Listen again. What three suggestions are rejected, and why?**

Suggestion	Why was it rejected?
1.	
2.	
3.	

UNIT 3

What exactly do you do?

Student CD Track: 6

A Listen and circle the best response.

1. a. I work in a bank.
   b. It's pretty tough.
   c. I'd like to be a doctor, I guess.

2. a. Around $45 thousand.
   b. I answer phones and type letters.
   c. I'm not sure.

3. a. Yeah, it's really involving.
   b. Oh, you know. An average amount.
   c. A lot of hard work.

4. a. Yeah, sometimes it's a little boring.
   b. Yeah, every day is different.
   c. Yeah, I love exciting work.

5. a. Pretty responsible, I guess?
   b. I can type 90 words a minute.
   c. I make coffee and collect mail.

6. a. Making the coffee!
   b. I'm not bad.
   c. I can't remember.

B Listen again and check your answers.

Student CD Track: 7

A Read the statements. Then listen and circle *T* for *True*, *F* for *False*, or *U* for *Unknown*.

1. Judy and Bill went to school together.   T   F   U
2. Judy is a newspaper reporter.   T   F   U
3. Judy got the job at a recruitment seminar.   T   F   U
4. Bill would like to be a reporter.   T   F   U

B Listen again. Check (✔) Judy's job responsibilities.

- ☐ turn on coffee machine
- ☐ turn on office equipment
- ☐ buy paper
- ☐ load machines with paper
- ☐ photocopy documents

- ☐ collect mail
- ☐ take lunch orders
- ☐ prepare lunch
- ☐ go on assignments

UNIT 4

It doesn't fit.

Student CD Track: 8

A Listen and circle the best response.

1. a. It's great.
   b. Can I come too?
   c. I'm not invited.

2. a. I haven't decided yet.
   b. Yeah, you should get a bigger pair.
   c. Yeah, maybe a little.

3. a. No, the legs are too tight.
   b. It's a bit too expensive.
   c. I'm not sure.

4. a. You're paying for the brand.
   b. Let's look for a more expensive one.
   c. That's a good idea.

5. a. The sleeves are too long.
   b. The collar is coming undone.
   c. I think the zipper is broken.

6. a. Yeah, it looks good.
   b. No, the hem is coming down.
   c. No, I don't like the legs.

B Listen again and check your answers.

Student CD Track: 9

A Listen and number in order the things that Sally talks about? One is extra.

○ _____ ○ _____ ○ _____ ○ _____

B Listen again. What is Sally's complaint about each item? Write the problem under the item.

UNIT

I'm not sure what it's called.

Student CD Track: 10

A **Listen and circle the best response.**

1. **a.** They're called chopsticks.
   b. They're called potholders.
   c. They're called toothpicks.

2. **a.** No, I'll just use a frying pan.
   b. No, I'll just use a can opener.
   c. No, I'll just use chopsticks.

3. **a.** The potholder's over there.
   b. The kettle's over there.
   c. The can opener's over there.

4. **a.** I'll get the kettle.
   b. I'll get the spatula.
   c. I'll get the cutting board.

5. **a.** OK, I'll have to find the can opener.
   b. OK, I'll have to find the chopsticks.
   c. OK, I'll have to find the corkscrew.

6. **a.** Yeah, we need to get a new frying pan.
   b. Yeah, we need to get a new chopping board.
   c. Yeah, we need to get a new kettle.

B **Listen again and check your answers.**

Student CD Track: 11

A **Listen and circle the best answer.**

1. **These people are planning . . .**
   a. a dinner party.
   b. a barbecue.
   c. a wedding.

2. **They are . . .**
   a. brother and sister.
   b. colleagues.
   c. husband and wife.

3. **They are probably going to eat . . .**
   a. at home.
   b. in a park.
   c. on a boat.

B **Listen again. Check (✔) the items they already have and cross (✗) the items they need to get.**

To bring:

☐ frying pan   ☐ knife
☐ spatula   ☐ glasses
☐ plates   ☐ corkscrew
☐ cutting board   ☐ can opener

I thought you spoke English!

UNIT **6**

TASK 1

Student CD Track: **12**

A Listen and circle the best response.

1. a. It's called a footpath.
   b. It's called a sidewalk.
   c. It's called a walkway.

2. a. They call it petrol
   b. They call it kerosene.
   c. They call it gas.

3. a. It's a plug.
   b. It's a tap.
   c. It's a plunger.

4. a. Yeah, it's called an elevator.
   b. Yeah, it's called a lift.
   c. Yeah, it's called a flat.

5. a. Yeah, it's the ground floor.
   b. Yeah, it's the first floor.
   c. Yeah, it's the second floor.

6. a. It's called a bonnet.
   b. It's called a boot.
   c. It's called a hood.

B Listen again and check your answers.

TASK 2

Student CD Track: **13**

A Read the statements. Then listen and circle *T* for *True*, *F* for *False*, or *U* for *Unknown*.

1. Rob stayed at a friend's house in London.   T   F   U
2. Rob went to London on business.   T   F   U
3. Rob has a daughter.   T   F   U
4. Rob and the other speaker work together.   T   F   U

B Listen again and number the pictures in the order Rob talks about them. Some are extra.

You'll buy anything.

Student CD Track: **14**

A Listen and circle the best response.

1. **a.** For exercising.
   b. Oh, I really don't think we need one.
   c. No, I think we should buy it.

2. **a.** Why, don't you think it's useful?
   b. What should we do?
   c. I think it's a waste of money.

3. **a.** I can use it well.
   b. It peels vegetables.
   c. It sure does.

4. **a.** I have no idea.
   b. It talks.
   c. You use them in your bathroom.

5. **a.** No, I think it would be quite useful.
   b. What for?
   c. It's for the shower.

6. **a.** A key finder.
   b. For finding keys.
   c. Thirty dollars.

B Listen again and check your answers.

Student CD Track: **15**

A Listen and circle the items that Lindy and Jack talk about.

You'll never lose your keys again. *The new gadget everybody wants!* ○	Enjoy music and privacy anywhere. *Made in America, by Americans!* ○	Makes hard work a thing of the past. *Uses new Ultra-Titanium technology!* ○
Perfect for overnight guest, or for camping. *As comfortable as sleeping in a luxury hotel!* ○	Cutting hair was never so easy. *No more embarrassing neck hair!* ○	Walk your way to a slimmer, fitter body. *As used by top TV stars!* ○

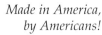

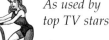

B Listen again. Put *L* next to the items Lindy wants, *J* next to the items Jack wants, and *B* next to the ones they both want.

UNIT

Our sales target is $1.1 million.

Student CD Track: 16

A Listen and circle the best response.

1. **a.** Japan.
   b. The United States.
   c. India.

2. **a.** The Moon.
   b. The Sun.
   c. Mars.

3. **a.** The Great Wall of China.
   b. The Taj Mahal.
   c. The Pyramids.

4. **a.** Angels.
   b. UFOs.
   c. Santa Claus.

5. **a.** Humans.
   b. Sheep.
   c. Rats.

6. **a.** One day.
   b. One week.
   c. One month.

B Listen again and check your answers.

Student CD Track: 17

A Listen and circle the best answer.

1. **This is a . . .**
   a. business meeting.
   b. casual conversation.
   c. job interview.

2. **Jim is talking to . . .**
   a. a junior coworker.
   b. an interviewer.
   c. his boss.

3. **They are talking about . . .**
   a. a sales conference.
   b. Jim's sales figures.
   c. a job vacancy.

B Listen again and check (✔) the correct graph.

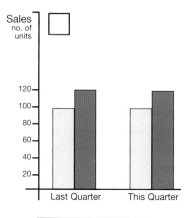

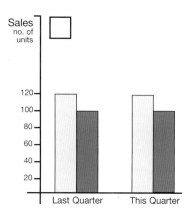

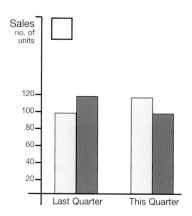

UNIT 9

I have a driving lesson tonight.

Student CD Track: 18

A Listen and circle the best response.

1. a. Sure, could I have your name and address?
   b. I'm afraid I can't.
   c. 9 a.m. to 5 p.m.

2. a. You passed your test.
   b. Tomorrow at three.
   c. Last night at seven.

3. a. Sure, for what time?
   b. OK, let me know if you change your mind.
   c. That's great news.

4. a. I'm not sure.
   b. I'm busy.
   c. OK, how about the day after?

5. a. It's beautiful.
   b. I'm afraid not.
   c. Not too bad.

6. a. No, it was a truck.
   b. I don't think so.
   c. Let me check.

B Listen again and check your answers.

Student CD Track: 19

A Listen. Number the notes on the tester's form in the order they occurred.

Tester's Report

Pass / Fail

Tester: _Pete Chalk_

Applicant: _Jackie Phillips_

Date: _12 June_

NOTES:

- *Nearly hit young woman crossing street.* _____

- *Turned wrong way down one way street.* _____

- *Got ticket from police.* _____

- *Hit post while backing out of parking lot.* _____

- *Scraped side of car on gate.* _____

B Listen again. The tester has made three mistakes in his notes. Circle the mistakes and write the correct information.

UNIT 10

She wants a seat to Miami.

TASK 1

Student CD Track: 20

A Listen and circle the best response.

1. a. Sure, your name, please?
   b. Sure, is next week OK?
   c. How about last week?

2. a. Next week.
   b. Two weeks ago.
   c. No, I'm coming back.

3. a. No, I'd like an aisle seat.
   b. No, I'm just on business.
   c. No, economy.

4. a. Is six OK?
   b. How about 2 a.m.?
   c. How about Kuala Lumpur?

5. a. It's British Airways.
   b. Yeah, I am.
   c. About two hours.

6. a. I'm not sure.
   b. Singapore Airlines.
   c. Yeah, that's right.

B Listen again and check your answers.

TASK 2

Student CD Track: 21

A Listen and circle the best answer.

1. Julie is talking to . . .
   a. her boss.
   b. a client.
   c. a travel agent.

2. Peter's first stop is . . .
   a. Hong Kong.
   b. Miami.
   c. Chicago.

3. He's going to Miami for . . .
   a. a meeting.
   b. a golf trip.
   c. a wedding.

B Listen again and fill in the information on the reservation form.

Planet Travel

Itinerary for Peter Tan

From	Destination	Date	Class
London	_____	_____	business/economy
_____	_____	_____	business/economy
_____	_____	_____	business/economy

How do I get downtown?

TASK 1 ## Student CD Track: 22

A Listen and circle the best response.

1. a. If I were you, I'd head downtown.
   b. Why don't you go, too?
   c. Well, you've got a couple of options.

2. a. A taxi would probably be fastest.
   b. Yes, I would.
   c. I'm not sure how long it takes.

3. a. Every five minutes or so.
   b. In that case, I'll drive.
   c. Yes, it's very frequent.

4. a. It takes about four hours.
   b. About 25 kilometers.
   c. Every couple of minutes.

5. a. Sure. What's your destination?
   b. Is there a taxi?
   c. What time is it?

6. a. Only for trains.
   b. On the fourth floor.
   c. Down this street, on the left.

B Listen again and check your answers.

TASK 2 ## Student CD Track: 23

A Read the statements. Then listen and circle *T* for *True*, *F* for *False*, or *U* for *Unknown*.

1. Joe and Nina are colleagues.   T   F   U
2. Nina is at a hotel.   T   F   U
3. Nina's flight was on time.   T   F   U
4. The meeting will take a long time.   T   F   U

B Read Nina's note. Listen again and correct any mistakes in the directions.

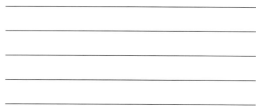

Directions to local office

exit baggage claim area and go straight

go straight up stairs into subway

take uptown train and get off at Broadway

go up stairs and turn left

take exit D

walk three blocks, building is straight ahead

take elevator to 60th floor

turn left after restrooms, meeting room is
at end of hall

_____
_____
_____
_____
_____
_____
_____
_____

UNIT **12**

Self-Study Practice

Is this where I get my student ID?

TASK **1**

Student CD Track: **24**

A Listen and circle the best response.

1. **a.** Oh, you need to go to the library.
   b. Oh, you need to go to the auditorium.
   c. Oh, you need to go to the finance office.

2. **a.** At the student affairs office.
   b. At the medical center.
   c. At the cafeteria.

3. **a.** The auditorium is over there.
   b. The student bookstore is over there.
   c. The financial office is over there.

4. **a.** OK, where's the bank?
   b. OK, where's the cafeteria?
   c. OK, where's the library?

5. **a.** I need to register for my class.
   b. I need to get something for my headache.
   c. I need to pay my student bills.

6. **a.** Some textbooks.
   b. You don't need anything.
   c. A check or credit card.

B Listen again and check your answers.

TASK **2**

Student CD Track: **25**

A Listen and circle the best answer.

1. **Richard is talking to . . .**
   a. his teacher.
   b. his mother.
   c. his friend.

2. **He is . . .**
   a. at university.
   b. at home.
   c. in a restaurant.

3. **How many of his tasks did he get done?**
   a. Two.
   b. Three.
   c. Four.

B Listen again. Check (✔) the things Richard managed to get done. For the things he didn't do, write the reasons why he couldn't.

- ☐ buy books for class
- ☐ pay for classes
- ☐ get student ID card
- ☐ get class schedule for semester
- ☐ register for classes

It's a really cool site.

Student CD Track: 26

Listen and circle the best response.

1. a. Hardly ever.
   b. For e-mail mostly.
   c. I can't remember.

2. a. It's expensive.
   b. I find it boring.
   c. It helps me keep in touch with people.

3. a. I don't.
   b. For listening practice.
   c. I like e-mailing people.

4. a. No, the server was down.
   b. No, it's expensive.
   c. No, from 6:00.

5. a. Not really.
   b. My friend's web site.
   c. I can't find the URL.

6. a. I have quite a few.
   b. E-mail.
   c. It's really useful.

B **Listen again and check your answers.**

Student CD Track: 27

A **Listen and check (✔) the web sites that Bernie visited today.**

Edit View Go **Bookmarks** **Communicator** Help
Add Bookmark ⌘D
Edit Bookmarks ⌘B
Guide ▶
getajob.org ☐
dailynews.com ☐
buymusic.com ☐
universityofla.edu ☐
californiabank.com ☐
findafriend.info ☐
free-email.net ☐

What did he do there?

_____

_____

_____

_____

_____

_____

_____

B **Listen again. Note what Bernie did at each site.**

UNIT

That's a good question.

Student CD Track: 28

A Listen and circle the best response.

1. a. The long hours.
   b. Meeting famous people.
   c. It's really interesting.

2. a. I saw an ad in the paper.
   b. About five years ago.
   c. I'm not sure.

3. a. It's a great career and I'd recommend it.
   b. Listen carefully to the interviewer's questions.
   c. Think about why you want to be an interviewer.

4. a. No, TV is great.
   b. No, I think a lot of children do.
   c. No, I think reading is better for them.

5. a. It makes me nervous.
   b. They love it.
   c. I'd like to be famous.

6. a. They're difficult topics, aren't they?
   b. Celebrities, definitely.
   c. Not very interesting.

B Listen again and check your answers.

Student CD Track: 29

A Listen and circle the best answer.

1. Carl used to be . . .
   a. Kate's coworker.
   b. Kate's boss.
   c. Kate's husband.

2. Kate asks Carl for . . .
   a. a job.
   b. money.
   c. advice.

3. Kate plans to . . .
   a. accept the job offer.
   b. refuse the job offer.
   c. think about it some more.

 Listen again. Note the pros and cons of being a news anchorperson.

Pros	Cons

TASK **1**

Student CD Track: **30**

A Listen and circle the best response.

1. **a.** Yeah, smoking in restaurants.
   b. Yeah, flying.
   c. Yeah, spiders really scare me.

2. **a.** I hate snakes.
   b. I can't stand people who litter.
   c. I don't really like loud music.

3. **a.** They don't bother me.
   b. I have a phobia.
   c. I've never tried it.

4. **a.** It doesn't bother me.
   b. Sorry about that.
   c. I had one too.

5. **a.** It really annoys me.
   b. I have a real phobia about it.
   c. I think it would be great.

6. **a.** Probably people who litter.
   b. Heights, definitely!
   c. I haven't decided yet.

B Listen again and check your answers.

TASK **2**

Student CD Track: **31**

A Listen and circle the best answer.

1. **Today is . . .**
   a. Saturday.
   b. Monday.
   c. Friday.

2. **Alison and June are . . .**
   a. sisters.
   b. coworkers.
   c. mother and daughter.

3. **They are . . .**
   a. at work.
   b. at home.
   c. at the supermarket.

B Listen again and fill in the chart. What is each person's problem, and what solutions are suggested?

		Problem	Solution
	June		
	Alison		

UNIT 16

That sounds dangerous!

TASK 1

Student CD Track: **32**

A Listen and circle the best response.

1. a. That sounds good. When?
    b. I'll think about it.
    c. Are you kidding? No way!

2. a. Really? How was it?
    b. But I can't drive.
    c. Sounds too scary for me.

3. a. Terrified!
    b. Exhausted!
    c. Thrilled!

4. a. I'm so nervous.
    b. I'm so jealous.
    c. I'm so excited.

5. a. Yeah, but rewarding.
    b. Yeah, it does sound easy.
    c. Yeah, but I prefer the jungle.

6. a. I think so, too.
    b. I'm terrified of heights.
    c. I'm jealous.

B Listen again and check your answers.

TASK 2

Student CD Track: **33**

A Read the statements. Then listen and circle *T* for *True*, *F* for *False*, or *U* for *Unknown*.

1. Mike and Sarah work together.	T	F	U
2. Mike and Sarah went on vacation together.	T	F	U
3. Sarah is afraid of heights.	T	F	U
4. Mike is going to take this trip next vacation.	T	F	U

B Read the advertisement. Listen again and check (✔) the activities Sarah did on her vacation. Note the reasons why she didn't do the other activities.

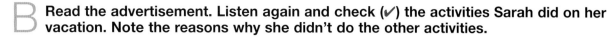

Two Weeks of Tropical Adventure!

Wild Travel's 14-day adventure trip to Wallaby Island includes:

- Wind surfing
- Scuba diving
- Bungee jumping
- Jungle trekking

- Parasailing
- Rock climbing
- Surfing
- Caving

Or, you can just lie on the beach, or party in one of our nightclubs! Call **Wild Travel** on **555-6343** for more details.

Self-Study Practice

UNIT 17

It has good points and bad points.

TASK 1

Student CD Track: 34

A Listen and circle the best response.

1. **a.** I'll think about it.
   b. Yeah, they are.
   c. I did. It's terrible.

2. **a.** I think you're right.
   b. Yeah, you will.
   c. I agree. It's a good idea.

3. **a.** No, but it will create jobs.
   b. Yes, it should.
   c. Yes, it has some disadvantages.

4. **a.** You think so?
   b. You don't think so?
   c. It's a tourist resort.

5. **a.** No, I'm in favor of it.
   b. No, I think you're wrong.
   c. No, not really.

6. **a.** No, I won't.
   b. I guess so.
   c. Yeah, I do.

B Listen again and check your answers.

TASK 2

Student CD Track: 35

A Read the statements. Then listen and circle *T* for *True*, *F* for *False*, or *U* for *Unknown*.

1. An amusement park is planned for Discovery Bay.	T	F	U
2. Rick heard about the news on TV.	T	F	U
3. Donna and Rick have been to an amusement park together.	T	F	U
4. Dolphins live in Discovery Bay.	T	F	U
5. Donna and Rick agree with each other.	T	F	U

B Listen again and write down Donna's and Rick's opinions.

Donna's Opinions	Rick's Opinions
_____	_____
_____	_____
_____	_____
_____	_____
_____	_____

UNIT 18

I was so embarrassed.

TASK 1

Student CD Track: 36

A **Listen and circle the best response.**

1. a. You must have felt really disappointed.
   b. You must have been really embarrassed.
   c. You must have been really frustrated.

2. a. Did he say thank you?
   b. Did he say excuse me?
   c. Did he say sorry?

3. a. I was so annoyed.
   b. I was really embarrassed.
   c. I was quite amused.

4. a. That's a funny story.
   b. How amusing!
   c. Yeah? What?

5. a. Yeah, you poor thing.
   b. Are you sure?
   c. I don't know.

6. a. Oh, how embarrassing.
   b. Oh, how disappointing.
   c. Oh, how frustrating.

B **Listen again and check your answers.**

TASK 2

Student CD Track: 37

A **Read the statements. Then listen and circle _T_ for _True_, _F_ for _False_, or _U_ for _Unknown_.**

1. Kate needed to go down to the storeroom.	T	F	U
2. It was lunchtime.	T	F	U
3. She decided to walk up the fire escape stairs.	T	F	U
4. All the doors were locked.	T	F	U
5. She took off her shoe to bang on the door.	T	F	U
6. When the door was opened, she felt happy.	T	F	U

B **Listen again and complete Kate's letter to her mother.**

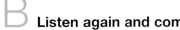

> _Dear Mum,_
>
> _You wouldn't believe what happened to me today. I was at work and . . ._
>
> _____
>
> _____
>
> _____
>
> _____
>
> _____

What's on TV tonight?

  Student CD Track: **38**

A **Listen and circle the best response.**

1. a. That's a good idea.
   b. I wouldn't mind.
   c. Anything is OK with me.

2. a. What time is it on?
   b. What channel's it on?
   c. What's on?

3. a. It's tonight.
   b. Yeah, it was on two weeks ago.
   c. No, I'm pretty sure it's the Stones.

4. a. I'm not interested in documentaries.
   b. I don't really like classical music.
   c. I don't really care much for dramas.

5. a. No, thanks. I'm not hungry.
   b. What time is it on?
   c. Sometimes. It depends.

6. a. I don't like music shows very much.
   b. Are you going?
   c. Oh, my radio is broken.

B **Listen again and check your answers.**

Student CD Track: **39**

A **Listen. What kinds of programs do you hear? Circle the correct answer for each.**

1.	news	sports	drama
2.	weather	travel	documentary
3.	quiz show	news	sports
4.	talk show	current affairs	business news
5.	travel	news	science program

 B **Listen again and note the main details you hear.**

1. _____
   _____

2. _____
   _____

3. _____
   _____

4. _____
   _____

5. _____
   _____

UNIT

I hear what you're saying.

TASK 1

Student CD Track: **40**

A Listen and circle the best response.

1. a. Really? How does he read?
   b. Does he know sign language?
   c. Does he use a wheelchair?

2. a. There's no such thing.
   b. It's delicious.
   c. It smells great.

3. a. There's an unusual texture.
   b. There's a strange scent.
   c. There's a weird sound.

4. a. It's too bitter, don't you think?
   b. It's too bright for me.
   c. It's a bit too loud.

5. a. Sorry, I couldn't hear you.
   b. Sorry, I don't agree.
   c. Sorry, I didn't see it.

6. a. Yeah, I can see much better now.
   b. Yeah, I think it probably is.
   c. Yeah, that feels great.

B Listen again and check your answers.

TASK 2

Student CD Track: **41**

A Listen and number the parts of the eye in the order the speaker talks about them.

_____ lens   _____ retina   _____ pupil

_____ cornea   _____ iris   _____ optic nerve

B Look at the diagram. Listen again and label the diagram using the words above.

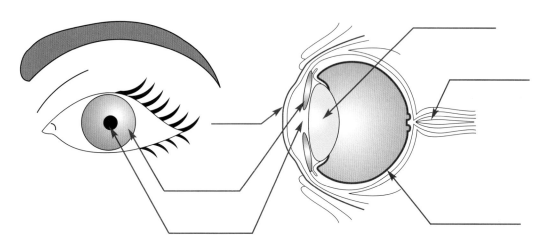

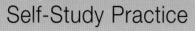

Track Listing

Track	Content	
1	Announcement	
2	Unit 1	Task 1
3	Unit 1	Task 2
4	Unit 2	Task 1
5	Unit 2	Task 2
6	Unit 3	Task 1
7	Unit 3	Task 2
8	Unit 4	Task 1
9	Unit 4	Task 2
10	Unit 5	Task 1
11	Unit 5	Task 2
12	Unit 6	Task 1
13	Unit 6	Task 2
14	Unit 7	Task 1
15	Unit 7	Task 2
16	Unit 8	Task 1
17	Unit 8	Task 2
18	Unit 9	Task 1
19	Unit 9	Task 2
20	Unit 10	Task 1
21	Unit 10	Task 2

Track	Content	
22	Unit 11	Task 1
23	Unit 11	Task 2
24	Unit 12	Task 1
25	Unit 12	Task 2
26	Unit 13	Task 1
27	Unit 13	Task 2
28	Unit 14	Task 1
29	Unit 14	Task 2
30	Unit 15	Task 1
31	Unit 15	Task 2
32	Unit 16	Task 1
33	Unit 16	Task 2
34	Unit 17	Task 1
35	Unit 17	Task 2
36	Unit 18	Task 1
37	Unit 18	Task 2
38	Unit 19	Task 1
39	Unit 19	Task 2
40	Unit 20	Task 1
41	Unit 20	Task 2

See pages 108–127 for the Self-Study Practice Tasks.